Janus Strategy is a gem of a book! It explores one of the eternal challenges in the field of strategy - how to manage dual and often contradictory challenges such as low cost and differentiation or centralisation and decentralisation simultaneously. Building on rigorous research and using a number of inspiring company examples, the book identifies the ingredients that need to be put together to meet this challenge. This superb book is full of fresh ideas and practical advice. It deserves to be widely read and be on the shelf of every senior executive crafting their organisation's strategy.

Costas Markides, Professor of Strategy & Entrepreneurship, Holder of the Robert Bauman Chair in Strategic Leadership, London Business School

Janus Strategy is a highly accessible and enjoyable practitioner's guide to ambidexterity: the ability to both explore and exploit in an advantaged manner. Illustrated by colorful case studies it argues that by deploying 6 principles, companies can not only trade off opposing considerations but achieve synergy between them, just as the Roman god Janus, was able to see in different directions simultaneously.

Martin Reeves, Senior Partner and Managing Director in the Boston Consulting Group's San Francisco office; Chairman of the BCG Henderson Institute

If you ever wondered how to pursue promising, though contradicting objectives (efficient operations and high risk innovation for example), this is a book for you. It's both an eye-opener and practical guide helping you to build your own Janus strategy. The stories from companies having done this before, makes it a great read. No doubt you will enjoy it as much as I did.

Christian Stadler, Professor of Strategy at WBS and author of Open Strategy, MIT Press

I have known and worked with Loizos Heracleous for many years and executive colleagues and corporate students have found his work to be both inspirational and of practical value. I trust readers will find this book equally stimulating.

Richard Hill, Director of Learning and Development at Rolls Royce (retired)

Bringing together a fascinating mix of cases, examples and thinking from refreshingly different areas, Heracleous has created a book that is as intriguing and inspiring as it is pragmatic and timely.

Marcus Alexander, Adjunct Professor of Strategy & Entrepreneurship at London Business School, Non-Executive Director and Strategy Consultant

Loizos is one of those very few academics who combines a joyful enthusiasm for business with rigorous research and analysis. Being able to handle ambiguity, to be able to think and chew gum, to be able to look and act in two different directions at the same time is a key skill of people who aspire to run large organizations, and is the reason why being a CEO can be such fun.

Rupert Soames OBE, Chief Executive Officer, Serco

A Janus himself as a rigorous researcher and inspiring educator at the same time, Loizos Heracleous has provided a much-needed perspective on strategy in his book *Janus Strategy*. Often managers shy away from trying to resolve paradoxes and conflicts in their business. This book shows us how to welcome and be comfortable with them, and more importantly, how to use them to build competitive advantage.

Pinar Ozcan, Professor of Entrepreneurship & Innovation, Saïd Business School, University of Oxford

Janus Strategy is a masterful presentation of the latest thinking about organization strategy written by one of the leading analysts and authorities on the subject. The book explains how strategy now requires multi-faceted thinking in today's complex world and illustrates the ideas with compelling case studies of leading corporations in different industries including: Apple, NASA, PARC, Singapore Airlines, and Xerox. Strategy-oriented executives, consultants, and business students will find this a richly rewarding read.

Robert J. Marshak, Ph.D., Distinguished Scholar-in-Residence Emeritus, School of Public Affairs, American University, and author of Dialogic Process Consulting: Generative Meaning-Making in Action

Heracleous inspires with a wonderful and rich collage of ideas drawn from Greek philosophers, Roman mythology, Nobel Laureates, and contemporary business leaders under the rubric of *Janus Strategy*. These insights on strategy are even more important in our digital age as we navigate uncertainty and crisis characteristic of our times.

Michael Barrett, Professor of Information Systems and Innovation Studies, Judge Business School, University of Cambridge

Janus Strategy
Published by KDP

ISBN: 9798678340917

Dedication

I dedicate this book to my parents who never questioned why
I wanted to spend my life in the world of ideas, and who
worked extremely hard so I could have the luxury to be
educated without having to worry where the next meal
would come from or who would pay the bills

Contents

Acknowledgements

I am grateful to the amazing colleagues and associates with whom I worked on research projects over the years, or who provided their thoughts on what I wrote. These include Jean Bartunek, Martin Friesl, Steven Gonzalez, Oliver Fischer, Angeliki Papachroni, Sotirios Paroutis, Christiane Prange, Irina Surdu, Douglas Terrier, Christina Wawarta and Jochen Wirtz. I am thankful that these colleagues took the journey of ideas with me or provided a critical eye on my work since they are exceptional scholars, executives, consultants or strategists (often more than one of these things at once). I am also grateful to the talented artist Telmo Ferreira for creating the illustrations

List of Tables

List of Figures

List of Illustrations

Janus strategy involves moves that accomplish dual
objectives simultaneously

Preamble

This book has been a long time in the making. I was sensitised to the dilemmas and inherent contradictions of business during my PhD research at Cambridge University between 1994 to 1997, when I had the opportunity to read Charles Hampden Turner's book Charting the Corporate Mind[1]. Charles argued that intractable challenges of strategy and organization can be expressed as dilemmas whose poles can be reconciled by finding ways to address and interrelate both poles, and that this reconciliation can provide strategic direction and competitive success. Inspired by what I started to see in some leading, successful companies through in-depth case research, by 2006 I wanted to work on a book on how these companies manage to have winning combinations of strategies and capabilities that had traditionally been considered distinct or mutually competing. In 2009 I presented a talk at Warwick Business School entitled "Quantum strategies and organizational resilience", based on this case research. I argued that the strategic orthodoxy as found in Harvard Professor's Michael Porter's work[2] in the 1970s and 1980s, that firms had to choose a single "generic strategy" of differentiation or cost leadership (combined with a choice of market scope), then align all their resources and operations behind that strategy to achieve sustainable advantage was most often sound advice; but not always. A clear choice of generic strategy gives direction on how to allocate resources, avoids potential conflicts across functions on such areas as values, processes and policies, and offers an unambiguous unique selling proposition to the market.

Yet, I thought that this strategic orthodoxy could be challenged. Alignment could potentially breed inertia, and there are ways to be both aligned and agile. Importantly, we can empirically see some organizations that have broken assumed trade-offs such as the one between quality and cost. My research of companies such as Singapore Airlines[3] and Apple[4] for example started pointing in this direction. Professor Porter had allowed that a combined strategy was possible, but only temporarily until competitors managed to imitate whatever competency was allowing such a strategy and then forced the firm to make a clear choice. Porter believed that a combined, integrated strategy that would encompass different "generic strategies" was not possible in the long term.

Others however started exploring how the inherent tensions of business could be negotiated. As early as 1976, Robert Duncan[5] argued that companies should have dual organization structures, each consistent with the particular stage of innovation the company was engaged in. In the initiation stage the structure should be more organic and flexible, and in the implementation stage the structure should be more mechanistic and defined. From 1988 onwards, Bartlett and Ghoshal proposed corporate "transnational" strategies[6] that combine the competing goals and tensions of global standardization as well as local customization. In 1991, James March[7] wrote about the importance of both exploiting current resources and capabilities and striving for efficiency, as well as simultaneously exploring new ones, innovating and opening up new markets. He termed this pursuit "ambidexterity". In 1999 Derek Abell[8] exhorted firms to balance competing in the present with developing capabilities for the future, labeling this orientation "dual strategy". By 2004, Costas Markides[9] advocated competing with dual business models at the corporate level, when different and often competing strategies are followed by different subsidiaries of the same corporation.

All of this pointed towards a new approach to strategy. Despite the valuable insights of this and related research, more needed to be done to understand how an organization could pursue strategies that encompass competing demands and capabilities simultaneously. This became painfully obvious during my executive education work over the years. This is where ideas and models need to be scalable up and down the ladder of abstraction[10]. High up on the ladder, sits the idea that a dual strategy or an ambidextrous company could simultaneously address a number of mutually competing demands. But how does this look at the more applied level of organizational choices, functional strategies and actions?

This is why I decided to conduct in-depth case research on companies that developed the capability to not only balance but rather synergize competing tensions. *Balancing* assumes a binary logic - more of X is less of Y, and a workable balance between them must be found. *Synergizing* however promotes a logic of synthesizing or integrating opposites and achieving virtuous-circles - more of X could also be more of Y, if we look beyond assumed constraints for novel solutions. I researched companies such as Singapore Airlines, Apple Inc, Narayana Hospital, Toyota and NASA that made great strides towards what I call *Janus strategy*. I also researched companies that tried to synergize competing tensions but were unsuccessful in doing so, such as Xerox. The label Janus Strategy was inspired by the Roman god Janus who faces in and is engaged with two, four or six opposing directions simultaneously. I am sharing in this book what I learned over this multi-year journey.

Icarus falling to his death while flying too close to the sun, a
stark warning on the risks of focusing too much on what led
to success and omitting to invest in new competencies

1

Be Like Janus

In the depths of antiquity, in mythical Greece, Perdix, sister of the inventor and architect Daedalus, sent her twelve-year-old son Talos to his uncle to apprentice. Talos proved to be a swift learner and ingenious as an inventor which made his uncle envious. Daedalus jealously threw Talos from the Acropolis and then made up a story that he accidentally fell. The goddess Minerva, who was fond of smart people, caught Talos mid-flight and turned him into a partridge. Nevertheless, Daedalus was banished from Athens for this misdeed. When he reached Crete with his son Icarus, the Cretan King Minos asked them to create a labyrinth where the half human, half beast Minotaur would be kept. The Minotaur was an abomination, but also the illegitimate son of Minos' wife Pasiphae, and a white bull that the god Poseidon had given Minos for the purposes of sacrifice.

Minos believed that his son Androgeus had been treacherously murdered in Athens and demanded as retribution that Athens sent 14 young men and women every nine years to feed the Minotaur. After the blood debt was paid twice, the Athenian King Theseus decided that the gory process had to stop. He decided to travel himself to Crete as part of the next sacrificial group to try and end Athens' blood payments. When he arrived in Crete Minos' daughter, Ariadne, fell in love with him and wanted to help him survive entering the labyrinth. So she consulted with Daedalus to find out more about the maze and gave Theseus a thread that he could use to find his way out. Theseus dispatched the Minotaur with the sword of his father, King Aegeus and made it out, using Ariadne's thread. When Minos found out what transpired he was incensed at Daedalus helping Ariadne. Theseus then eloped from Crete with Ariadne, which further angered Minos, so he decided to keep Daedalus and Icarus hostage on the island.

That is when Daedalus decided to construct wings held together with wax so he and his son would escape through flight to Sicily. The Roman poet Ovid, born in 47 BC, recounts[1] that after the pair successfully flew into the heavens, Icarus "began to rejoice in his bold flight and, deserting his leader, led by a desire for the open sky, directed his course to a greater height. The scorching rays of the nearer sun softened the fragrant wax which held his wings. The wax melted; his arms were bare as he beat them up and down, but, lacking wings, they took no hold on the air. His lips, calling to the last upon his father's name, were drowned in the dark blue sea, which took its name from him".

This cautionary tale reminds us that often companies get carried away with what made them successful. They focus on what they see as their strength, aligning investments, processes and values behind that strength, in a way that that over time fosters a narrow view of the world. They omit to build new competencies, challenge the status quo and embed diversity in their thinking. It is only a matter of time before their strength impedes learning and adaptation and becomes a millstone that drags them down as in the story of Icarus. This is what has been labeled the Icarus paradox[2], that occurs when one's greatest strength becomes a fatal weakness. This is a recognized strategic risk, that can be brought about by competency traps[3]. These traps occur when companies build and invest over time in a particular competency, at the expense of developing new, potentially useful ones.

What can be done to mitigate this risk? Janus, the Roman god simultaneously surveying different directions, offers us a hint. Companies have to be able to focus on the present and also on the future[4]; on exploiting and optimizing current resources and strengths and also opening up strategic options by developing and exploring new ones[5]; on what is happening daily in their particular competitive terrain and also how this terrain is shifting or even disappearing over the longer term. In short, they need to be like Janus.

Who is Janus?

Janus is the Roman god of beginnings and endings, past and future, transitions, boundaries, and gateways. As a liminal god[6], Janus operates between and across domains and holds the key to these domains. In one hand he holds a staff to point the way ahead; in the other he holds a key to open and close passageways. Janus is portrayed as having two heads (or four or six, depending on the number of sides of the relevant Roman dwelling) facing towards and presiding over opposite directions at the same time.

The paradoxical representation of Janus as simultaneously surveying opposite directions invites the realization that competing ideas or contradictions can co-exist and function together as one. This is not just an abstract statement. Organizations struggle with competing demands on a daily basis and with dilemmas where both sides have a legitimate claim. They include for example how to optimize operations through standard operating procedures, while at the same time maintaining flexibility and pursuing innovation; how to become as efficient as possible through cost reduction, while at the same time maintaining quality; how to empower employees while at the same time controlling performance; how to differentiate across functions while at the same time ensuring cross-functional cooperation and coordination. The list goes on. Rather than be blind to organizational contradictions, there are benefits to acknowledging and engaging with them. The interaction of opposites can be generative in one's thinking, pointing towards workable solutions to intractable dilemmas and creating sparks of insight. The generative power of paradoxes has been supported by research on themes such as paradoxical cognition, ambidextrous thinking, and leadership effectiveness[7].

Janus is not just any god. Out of the whole Roman pantheon, shaped by the Greek gods who commonly had their doppelgangers in the Roman culture, Janus was uniquely Roman. He had no Greek counterpart and even possibly once existed on the mortal plane in the form of a mythical King of Latium, a region in central Italy[8]. Janus had been part of Roman culture centuries before the Greek influence of the 2nd and 3rd centuries BCE. As an ancient animistic spirit, Janus inhabited gateways and arches; in the same way that Vesta inhabited the hearth, Penates the pantry and Lares Familiares the land[9].

Janus was ubiquitous in Roman ceremonies and rituals. Since he was the gatekeeper to the heavens one had to invoke and make offerings to Janus before they could commune with any other god, even Jupiter. Ceremonies dedicated to Janus were conducted by the highest priest, the King of the Sacred Rites, or *rex sacrorum*. Janus was referred to as the god of gods; he was the first of the gods and thus their father (the Ianuspater). As a god of beginnings, he was present when the world began and his blessing was sought in new endeavors. As an embodiment of opposites, he is generative. As a liminal spirit that can see in both the past and the future and in all directions simultaneously, he can control time and space. Knowledge of the future meant that Janus was evoked as a divinator, called upon to deliver good fortune when initiating military and other endeavors, and requested to grant desired omens. Janus stood between the mortals and the gods in conveying human prayer towards the heavens and divine omens towards earth.

Contradictions as a Condition of Existence

The ideas that Janus embodies, particularly the interaction of opposites and contradictions existing simultaneously within the same entity, are as old as time. Surviving literature and art in Asian and African civilizations portray gods with similar or equivalent powers. The Taoist view of the universe as arising from the continuous interweaving of yin (dark, hard) and yang (soft, light) energy has pervaded Chinese philosophy. The Zoroastrian concepts of Asha (order, truth) and Druj (disorder, deceit) are cornerstones of that religion. Heraclitus, the pre-Socratic paradoxical philosopher, shared similar messages in his work On Nature, that only survives in fragments: "Unite whole and part, agreement and disagreement, accordant and discordant; from all comes one, and from one all"[10]. Janus is the most prominent god in Western mythology to embody such attributes.

The fundamental dualities and contradictions of life often manifest in pathological ways. In literature, The Strange Case of Dr Jekyll and Mr Hyde written over a century ago by Robert Louis Stevenson[11] has become a classic. It is worth asking why this particular novel has become embedded in popular culture. It shows not only the internal, everlasting contradictions of human nature, but also in this case a pathological manifestation of these contradictions. Dr Jekyll, as he tries to make sense of the tensions within himself, and in trying to conceal from the world his indulgence in his guilty pleasures, reflects: "It was thus rather the exacting nature of my aspirations than any particular degradation in my faults that made me what I was, and, with even a deeper trench than in the majority of men, severed in me those provinces of good and ill which divide and compound man's dual nature … Though so profound a double-dealer, I was in no sense a hypocrite ; both sides of me were in dead earnest; I was no more myself when I laid aside restraint and plunged in shame than when I labored, in the eye of day, at the furtherance of knowledge or the relief of sorrow and suffering".

Another pathological manifestation of fundamental dualities and contradictions is the pervasive nature and nefarious uses of Barnum statements. PT Barnum led a varied and eventful life; he was a politician, businessman, author and philanthropist. He is best known for his Barnum & Bailey Circus and for his museums, in which he displayed human curiosities and hoaxes such as the "Feejee Mermaid", made of the top half of a monkey sewn onto the bottom half of a fish. Barnum believed that it was fine to create hoaxes as long as the public was entertained: "If I have exhibited a questionable dead mermaid in my Museum, it should not be overlooked that I have also exhibited cameleopards, a rhinoceros, grisly bears, orang-outangs, great serpents, etc., about which there could be no mistake because they were alive; and I should hope that a little 'clap-trap' occasionally, in the way of transparencies, flags, exaggerated pictures, and puffing advertisements, might find an offset in a wilderness of wonderful, instructive, and amusing realities. Indeed I cannot doubt that the sort of 'clap-trap' here referred to, is allowable, and that the public like a little of it mixed up with the great realities which I provide."[12]

Psychologists have long studied Barnum statements[13], which are statements that are true for most people but presented as being custom-made or tailored to particular individuals in order to deceive individuals into believing that the person speaking these statements has insights from mysterious or unusual sources. Barnum statements are essential to the work of magicians, mediums, astrologers, hoaxers, and fraudsters of all types. A central type of Barnum statement is one framing oppositions or contradictions as residing in the same person, such as: "you enjoy meeting your friends, but at the same time seek your own space; you very much love your family but sometimes loathe them; you find pleasure in travelling but cannot wait to return home". In another pathological manifestation of inherent dualities and contradictions, such statements take advantage of the human condition to convince gullible individuals of a fraudster's special, even mystical, insights.

Despite the above unfortunate uses of dualities, Janus represents a positive and productive way to conceive and deal with the tensions and contradictions that are inherent in life and organizations. We will use Janus as an inspiration and as a generative force for understanding how some organizations can simultaneously pursue opposing demands and excel in competing capabilities; and thus enjoy the spoils of success on the competitive battlefield. One label for the capability of attending to opposing demands simultaneously, is organizational ambidexterity. There is a significant and growing amount of research showing clear correlations between ambidexterity and organizational performance[14].

Janusian Thinking

The Harvard psychiatrist Albert Rothenberg has been researching what he calls Janusian thinking[15] for over five decades. He showed that such thinking has been central to creative endeavors by outstanding artists, authors and scientists. Such thinking has given birth to paradigm-shifting and field-birthing insights by Nobel laureates and fathers of science including Einstein, Darwin and Bohr.

Rothenberg defined Janusian thinking as "the capacity to conceive and utilize two or more opposite or contradictory ideas, concepts or images simultaneously"[16]. The simultaneity aspect and the continued juxtaposition of opposites rather than collapsing or reducing a dilemma in terms of an either/or choice, are central elements and help to distinguish Janusian thinking from other forms such as the Hegelian dialectic. Dialectic involves a process of thesis, antithesis, and synthesis, a sequential rather than a simultaneous process. Further, a state of synthesis in dialectic implies that the competing forces have been integrated and tamed rather than being maintained in a state of generative tension.

Rothenberg aimed to understand the links between Janusian thinking and creativity. He defined creations as "products which are both new and valuable", and creativity as the "capacity or state which brings forth creations"[17]. His clinical, documentary and experimental evidence over five decades points to robust connections between flashes of insight that give birth to or redefine entire scientific fields or create magnificent works of art, and Janusian thinking.

Darwin for example conceived of the idea of natural selection when re-reading Malthus's treatise on how uncontrolled population growth, within an environment with fixed resources, would inevitably lead to the extinction of the species. Darwin thought that such a struggle for existence could have both unfavorable (extinction) as well as favorable (adaptation) consequences, juxtaposing two opposing sets of ideas simultaneously. This train of thinking implied the possibility of variations over time that could be adaptive or maladaptive, leading to the concept of natural selection[18].

A crucial insight that helped Einstein move towards his general idea of relativity was when he realized that a person could be both falling and at rest at the same time, depending on the perspective one adopts. Since in a vacuum all objects fall at the same rate, a falling person who released some objects during their fall would not realize that these objects were falling since they would move at the same rate as the person. This person, from their perspective, could reasonably believe they were at rest; but from a different vantage point they would be falling. Einstein described this paradoxical insight, that a person could be falling and at rest at the same time, as the happiest thought of his life because it led him to his initial insights on relativity[19].

Bohr reached his complementarity principle when he realized that light and electrons can behave both like waves and like particles, depending on the experimental setting. Whereas at a larger scale the particle and wave behaviors are incompatible, and cannot be observed together, a fuller understanding of how light and electrons behave at the atomic level requires both perspectives. As he noted in a groundbreaking article in Nature[20] "The two views of the nature of light are rather to be considered as different attempts at an interpretation of experimental evidence ... The individuality of the elementary electrical corpuscles [particles] is forced upon us by general evidence. Nevertheless, recent experience ... requires the use of the wave theory superposition principle ... Just as in the case of light, we have consequently ... to face an inevitable dilemma ... here again we are not dealing with contradictory but with complementary pictures of the phenomena".

In all these and a plethora other cases that Rothenberg studied, in crucial stages of the emergence of creative, groundbreaking insights in science or influential works of literature and art, Janusian thinking was involved. This manifested as a conception of opposites that are seen to be essential to the subject under consideration, coming together. The realization that opposites are different, simultaneous aspects of the same phenomenon may not always make it into the final theory since theories have to be stated in more straightforward, testable terms, but it is inherent to understanding the inner workings of the topic and is what sparks novel insights.

Janus' Gift: From Motivation and Deviation to Gaining Insights

As part of a broader research project that encompassed structured interviews, experimental studies and documentary analysis, Rothenberg interviewed 22 Nobel prize laureates to better understand the creative process over time[21]. He identified four phases in the overall process of creation. First, there has to be *motivation to create*. All interviewees mentioned that they had consciously wanted to create new solutions, rather than to re-evaluate or extend existing ones; and that this process was often a very emotional one. Scientists had felt frustrated, they had suffered during the search, and when they finally reached their insights they felt elated and often basked in a sense of aesthetic beauty. All interviewees also referred to the benefits of coming with a fresh mindset into a field, being able to approach challenges without being too constrained by received wisdom of how one should look at and investigate things, so that novel perspectives could emerge.

Complementing the motivation to create, the second phase of the Janusian process is *deviation or separation from accepted rules, areas of focus, how these areas are defined, or how they are studied*. On the one hand, received wisdom can be helpful. It aids theory extension and knowledge accumulation within a process of normal science[22]. On the other hand however, it does not necessarily support paradigmatic change in terms of redirecting inquiry or reconceptualizing areas of inquiry. In fact, knowing how things have always been thought about or done can be a barrier to transformative insights. In phase two, key building blocks of what will eventually be fleshed out as a new theory are developed.

Initial insights from phase two then become inputs for the third phase, where the crux of Janusian thinking occurs; the *simultaneous bringing together of opposites in creative tension*. This is where Einstein realized that a falling man could be both in motion and at rest at the same time depending on perspective, Darwin that variations could be adaptive or destructive, and Bohr that light and electrons could behave both as particles and as waves at the atomic level, even though such behaviors are incompatible and could never in fact be observed together. Rothenberg's phase 3 may be an instance of what Arthur Koestler called "bisociation". In his Act of Creation[23], Koestler coined this term to describe the process of previously unrelated ideas coming together and forming something new. He noted that "the creative act consists in combining previously unrelated structures in such a way that you get more out of the emergent whole than you have put in … The bisociative act means combining two different sets of rules, to live on several planes at once". These insights often appear unexpectedly, seemingly out of nowhere. They may be the result of subconscious cognitive processing, informed by long periods of prior conscious reflection[24].

Phase four is the *elaboration of insights and the creation of theory*, a long and arduous process that involves linear argumentation, hypothesis development and experimental protocol. The oppositional qualities that spurred earlier insights may not be obvious in the elaborated theory, since scientific theories have to be expressed in ways that are predictive and testable. Any inherent contradictions may be ironed out in the way the theory is expressed. As Rothenberg notes, "It is in this construction phase that the structure of simultaneous opposition is modified, often to a point at which antitheses and apparent contradictions disappear completely. … by and large, stepwise logic and external validation dictate their elaborated content"[25].

Why does all of this matter? First, we know from Rothenberg's studies and related research in psychology and organization theory that Janusian thinking is not just another type of mindset; rather, it is crucial to gaining ground-breaking insights and in the case of organizations, effective strategic leadership. Second, organizations have to grapple with endemic, competing tensions and need to be ambidextrous; a capability that once developed can lead to higher performance. Third, ambidextrous capabilities and organizational configurations can support winning strategies, what we call here Janus strategies.

Einstein realizes someone can be stationary and falling at the same time, a defining insight for his relativity theory, on what he referred to as the happiest day of his life. An example of how groundbreaking insights can emerge from the generative nature of contradictions

The Roman god Janus looks simultaneously in two
directions. With one hand he holds a staff to show the way,
with the other a key to open and close passageways. Janus
embodies contradiction and paradox as generative forces in
all areas of life including commerce

2

Toward Janus Strategy

In 1996, when Indian cardiac surgeon Dr Shetty treated Mother Teresa, founder of the Missionaries of Charity and Nobel Peace Prize winner for her work with the poor, he learned a valuable lesson. This lesson would inspire him to set up Narayana Health and save the life of thousands of heart patients in India who would otherwise have died without access to proper, affordable medical care. What she told him was that "hands that serve are holier than lips that pray". At the time, Dr. Shetty was working in another hospital in India and was witnessing too many people lose their loved ones because they could not afford the cost of heart surgery that was equivalent of several years' salary in India.

The need for improved medical provision and infrastructure in India was and remains dire. There are 7 hospital beds per 10,000 population in India as compared to 63 beds in Europe, 34 beds in the USA, 25 beds in China and a world average of 26[1]. Only 3% of specialist physicians in India serve the rural population, that comprises 70% of India's total population. 61% of the costs of medical treatment in India are out-of-pocket, the highest percentage globally. Dr Shetty decided to build a hospital with a difference, with funds borrowed from his father-in-law. His mission was to provide quality, affordable cardiac healthcare to the masses[2].

Narayana Health (NH) Group's flagship hospital, with 300 beds, was founded in 2001 in the outskirts of Bangalore. Its mission was to serve everyone in need of medical care, including the poor and underprivileged who could not afford to pay. Narayana Health has grown to 47 healthcare facilities with over 6,500 beds, 30 specialties, and 17,000 employees[3]. It has lower operating costs and charges lower prices to patients than any other hospital chain in the world. The cost of open-heart surgery at NH for example is US$ 2,000[4]. This is much lower than the average cost in Indian hospitals of US$ 7,900, and about one sixtieth (yes, 1/60th) of the cost of open-heart surgery in the US, where the cost is in the region of US$ 100,000 to US$ 125,000. NH's ultimate goal is to keep increasing its operating efficiency so that it will at some point be able to offer open heart surgery at a cost of US$800. The Table below gives further comparative data[5].

Intriguingly, while NH's costs and prices charged are the lowest in the world, the quality of care is world class when seen via key indicators. The 30-day post-surgery mortality rate for a coronary bypass procedure at NH's Bangalore hospital for example is 1.3%, below the average rate of 1.9% in the United States. Infection rates for coronary bypass graft surgery are 1%, equal to that of the United States. NH's flagship center has grown to become a 3,000-bed multi-specialty "Health City" hospital comparable to the world's best.

Metric	Narayana Health	Industry
Cost of cardiac bypass surgery	US$ 2,000 in 2019 and reducing over time	US$ 7,900 in India, US$ 123,000 in US
30-day mortality rate for coronary bypass graft surgery	1.4%	1.9% in US
Infection rate for coronary bypass graft surgery	1%	1% in US
Bedsores	Almost 0%	8 to 40% globally
Installed cost per bed	US$ 43,000	US$ 60,000 in India
Number of cardiac surgeries per day per hospital	34	5 to 6 in India and US
Number of surgeries per surgeon	30 per week, 36,000 in career (25 years at 48 weeks per year)	India: 15 per week, 18,000 in career. US: 3-4 per week, 3,600-4,800 in career
Utilization of operating theatre	18 hours per day (15 min turnarounds)	8 hours per day (30 min turnarounds)

Table 2.1. Operational metrics at Narayana Health vs Industry

Dr Shetty's dedication to helping others as well as business acumen have been recognized over the years by numerous international awards. Yet he remains humble, true to the lesson he received from Mother Teresa about the importance of hands that heal, and has instilled this culture throughout NH: "I am essentially a heart surgeon who loves operating for the whole day if given a choice. I do spend about ten percent of my time every day on strategies, and day-to-day management of all our organization is left to the professionals. We do have senior doctors at key roles in the administration; however, they too spend most of their time in patient care and have associates who do the day-to-day management."[6]

NH achieves economies of scale, scope and learning. With higher scale, come lower average costs. The company does not acquire the latest medical technology, but rather reliable, tried and tested machines, and sweats the assets. Economies of learning come from honing skills over time. Doctors' skills and efficiency improve with the high volume of surgeries, and there are weekly meetings to share and best practices in the context of lean philosophy. Economies of scope come from sharing resources across units, for example having centralized diagnostic equipment and centrally coordinated purchasing. But these different types of economies are not sufficient to explain how NH manages to deliver high quality surgery at the lowest cost. There is a configuration of practices, that together form Janus strategy, as shown below.

Align but embrace paradox	NH achieves economies of scale, scope and learning through mutually supporting, standardized processes, leading to the lowest costs and prices in the world; at the same time as it delivers world class quality. High levels of standardization and reliability are coupled with continuous improvement and refinement
Be a Janus strategist	Founder Devi Shetty's vision is to offer surgeries at both high quality and at the lowest cost. He continues to be hands-on, conducting daily surgeries, as well as thinking strategically about the future of NH. Shetty's passion and vision touches all employees about what matters; helping society as well as creating a commercially viable, financially healthy business
Make dual strategic moves	NH develops a culture of thrift through processes such as sterilizing and reusing consumables and hiring in-house mechanics to maintain and fix old equipment. Company hires employees that believe in the vision and exert discretionary effort. NH developed its own Health Colleges to train nurses and physicians so as to ensure steady, high quality supply of personnel
Use tech to both exploit and explore	NH develops technology such as custom apps that connect patient records with central servers in real time, generating daily profit and loss account, adopting single-line billing for patients, Atma software that enables visibility and control of daily operations. These both optimize, as well as contribute to reliability of processes and quality of care
Design agile organization	Flat organization design, minimal bureaucracy, continuous efforts for improvement and sharing of best practices. Ongoing process innovations such as role enrichment for nurses and family challenge convention
Leverage business networks	NH develops and works in the long term with networks of local suppliers for quality inputs at lower cost. In this way it ensures reliability of the supply chain, high quality levels, and cost control. It owns and operates a network of 47 healthcare facilities with nearly 6,000 operational beds, allowing it achieve economies as well as transfer of learning

Table 2.2. The six elements of Janus strategy at Narayana Health

The six elements in Table 2.2 indicate that NH is an archetype of Janus strategy; an organization that can synergize the seemingly incompatible goals of intense efficiency ("cost leadership" among its peer group to use the established language of Porter's generic strategies), as well as world class quality levels ("differentiation" in the traditional strategy parlance). This is accomplished by an interconnected set of strategic innovations in terms of its business model and by precise, clockwork-like operations.

Janus strategy at NH creates a competitive advantage; as well as a noteworthy contribution to society that saves lives every day. NH is just one of a select breed of companies that manage not just to optimize and balance, but rather to synergize strategic goals that have traditionally been in tension with each other.

Optimization refers to maximizing outputs by achieving balance between fixed constraints and incompatible goals; where more of X is less of Y, and vice versa. To synergize however, means to find ways to transcend incompatibilities, to find virtuous circles, to reach a ground where two plus two can equal five; where X and Y can grow together. This is a very challenging strategy to achieve. One way it has been investigated is to see how many companies can outperform their peers on both revenue growth and profitability, goals that pose competing pressures. Significant investment is needed to grow, which reduces profitability in the short term. Conversely, cost reduction can lead to higher profitability in the short term; but compromise future growth and profits by starving growth-oriented investments.

McKinsey consultants investigated how many companies out of their sample of 1,077 could outperform in terms of revenue growth and net profit margin over a ten-year period. They found that 2.8% of companies outperformed in terms of growth, and 9.2% in terms of profitability. But only 0.8% of companies outperformed in both profit and growth[7]. The Boston Consulting Group asked the same question and found that only 2% of companies in their sample of 2,500 companies could accomplish this feat over a 5-year timeframe[8]. These rare companies can thus balance exploitation of current capabilities and resources with the exploration for new ones.

In this book we explore how organizations such as Narayana Health, Toyota, Singapore Airlines, Apple, and NASA, have accomplished different types of Janus strategy.

What is Janus Strategy?

Conventional strategy wisdom based on Professor Michael Porter's writings[9] from the 1970s and 1980s holds that firms should choose a single, clear "generic" strategy. This could be a strategy of "differentiation" (claiming uniqueness in their market positioning about quality, innovation, styling, or engineering, and also displaying such uniqueness); or a focus on "cost leadership" within a peer group via intense efficiency. This choice is combined with either serving a specific market niche better than established competitors or going for a broad market. Each company could then build on this initial, generic strategy through particular operational and positioning choices to align operations to strategy. According to Porter, trying to accomplish both cost leadership and differentiation would lead to operational confusion and to becoming "stuck in the middle" without any competitive advantage. Such an effort would run into organizational contradictions, stakeholder confusion, unclear positioning and ultimately would fail. The need to make tough strategic choices has been one of Porter's central claims, and it has shaped the field of strategy since[10]. This is good advice for many companies and situations, but does not take into account how technology, novel organization designs, the sharing economy, flexible employment contracts, and other developments can create opportunities to transcend tensions and synergize competing demands.

We know through empirical observation and in-depth case research that some extraordinary firms can accomplish Janus strategy, the ability to synergize capabilities and strategic positions that are traditionally considered contradictory or distinct. While Singapore Airlines for example is the most awarded airline in the world in terms of service excellence and innovation, it also manages to maintain intense control of its costs and maintain higher efficiency than its peers[11].

Apple has created market-defining innovations in terms of product design and integration of technologies, as well as perfecting the ecosystem business model of consumer electronics, software and services. What is not widely appreciated is that it also has the lowest costs compared to its peers, for example in terms of its SGA ratio (Sales, General and Administrative Costs) and its R&D intensity (Research & Development) ratio. Apple spends around 5% of revenues on R&D, lower than all its peers, and gets the highest bang for the buck in terms of what it can create with this spend. It also has the lowest bureaucratic costs, the costs of running an organization structure, since compared to its size, it has the flattest organization design in the industry[12].

Chinese enterprises such as Haier are disrupting Western multinationals by being able to offer both high technology and high variety at low cost, and by being able to move premium products into the mass market[13]. These capabilities are blurring and challenging what traditionally have been regarded as clear strategic lines. For example, the beliefs that high quality and variety comes at a cost penalty or a premium price; and that premium products cannot be mass marketed because their high costs imply a high price point that the mass market cannot bear.

While investigating the strategies and capabilities of the companies discussed in this book, two things became clear to me. First, that their accomplishments challenge the strategic orthodoxy that choosing one strategy precludes another because of the need for alignment and the existence of opportunity costs and sunk investments. What we see in these companies is that they simultaneously occupy strategic positions that have been considered contradictory or distinct. Second, having the capability to synergize competing demands can lead to competitive advantage that is relatively sustainable in a world where advantage is fleeting, because such a capability cannot be easily imitated. I label this pursuit Janus strategy and I explore the underlying principles involved in accomplishing it. These principles are based on in-depth case research on such companies.

Before settling on the term Janus strategy, I previously used the term quantum strategy[14] to describe such a capability. In quantum physics a particle can be at two places at the same time, an event deemed impossible at the conventional level of reality. In quantum computing, a quantum bit or qubit can be simultaneously in the position of zero and one. According to the CEO of a quantum computing company, "this object is actually in two different states at the same time. And it's not like it's half in this state and half in the other; it's in those two states at the same time ... Einstein called it spooky. But it is a fundamental law of quantum mechanics..."[15]. I employed this event as an analogy to describe the capability of an organization to occupy two competing strategic positions at once since strategically, it's at two places at the same time. I then decided that Janus strategy could more clearly convey this strategic approach.

It is worth noting that Janus strategies do not simply balance or optimize conflicting tensions within an assumption of a zero-sum game, or either/or thinking (that more of X is less of Y and vice versa). Rather, there has to be both/and thinking and actions. According to the Boston Consulting Group, "incumbents in uncertain and dynamic environments must simultaneously run the business by exploiting existing opportunities and reinvent the business by exploring new growth areas. This ambidexterity is especially difficult for large, established companies, which tend to overestimate the longevity of their business models. Those that do take exploratory steps often don't go far enough[16]"

Yet, strategic ambidexterity is still not at the level of Janus strategy. As shown in Figure 2.1 below, Janus strategies derive from sustainable outperformance in both dimensions of a dilemma, and on finding virtuous circles and ways to synergize the competing demands posed by the dilemma. So for example Narayana Health provides life-saving heart surgery at $1/60^{th}$ the cost of the same surgery in the United States, offering similar or higher levels of quality on key metrics relating to post-operative mortality and infection. Apple Inc. spends less than 5% of its revenues on Research and Development, as compared to other technology giants that spend several multiples of that amount; yet Apple has created market-defining products, regularly tops innovation rankings, and remains one of the most valuable companies in the world. Singapore Airlines has low costs relative to peers; yet is the most awarded airline in the world for service excellence and innovation; and has achieved healthy returns and comparative out-performance in an industry that bleeds red ink.

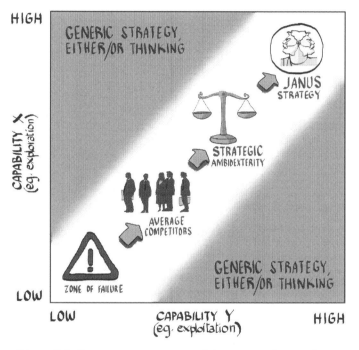

Figure 2.1: Janus strategy as synergizing competing tensions

Toward Janus Strategy

Competing tensions are endemic, embedded in the very fabric of organizations. Companies have for instance to both exploit current capabilities and resources, and at the same time explore, to develop new capabilities and resources[17]. They have to both perform in the present, as well as open up new avenues for the future[18]. Global companies have to standardize their processes and operations as far as possible across nations to accomplish efficiency and reliability; but also to customize their operations and offerings in different regions to suit the local conditions. At the level of organization design, companies have to differentiate their functions so that specialization and deep expertise can develop. At the same time they must also integrate their functions so that the overall mission can be delivered. At the individual, human level, companies have to empower their staff to ensure that employees give their best, but also have control over outputs to ensure quality and productivity. The list is endless. And such tensions repeat themselves, much like fractal patterns, throughout the organization.

Janus Strategies encompass generative tensions between opposites. They promote a way of thinking, as well as organizational principles, that seek to synergize competing tensions, create virtuous circles, and search for complementary solutions, rather than capitulating to the dilemmas and satisficing with binary, either/or solutions. This book outlines how Janus Strategy can be accomplished, based on insights from companies that have done so.

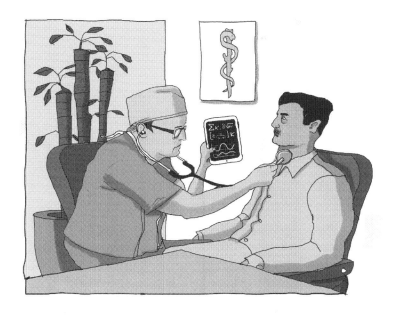

Dr Devi Shetty, founder of Narayana Health, examines a patient while keeping an eye on real-time hospital metrics. His insights and vision on the possibility of integrating intense efficiency, reliability and standardization in healthcare with world-class health outcomes, and his outstanding leadership and role modelling to accomplish this, led to creating an organization that saves thousands of lives that would otherwise have been lost, and does so on a commercially sustainable basis

3

The Six Elements

There are no fixed recipes that guarantee the accomplishment of Janus strategy or any other challenging strategy. The very existence of such recipes would make sustainable competitive advantage impossible, since anything that can be imitated by competitors becomes strategically banal and widespread and is not an advantage any longer. What we can have however is a list of ingredients, that mixed in terms of the right proportions and supported by the right processes, given key aspects of the competitive and task situations, can help the company accomplish groundbreaking strategies. There are six elements that I found to be crucial to accomplishing Janus strategy. There is no immutable formula on exactly what aspect of these elements, and how, they should be integrated. This is where leadership ingenuity and skill come in and this is all as it should be. What has become clear to me however is that these elements work together in virtuous circles, and if a single element is missing, the recipe may be spoiled.

From Generic Strategies to Synergizing Competing Demands[1]

Janus Strategy is unconventional and hard to imitate by competitors; this is why it is valuable in the competitive game. Such a strategy turns several traditional strategic assumptions on their head. Let's begin by looking at the traditional view of strategy. Michael Porter[2] argued that "the fundamental basis of above-average performance in the long run is sustainable competitive advantage ... there are two basic types of competitive advantage a firm can possess: low cost or differentiation ... combined with the scope of activities for which a firm seeks to achieve them lead to three generic strategies ... Each of the generic strategies involves a fundamentally different route to competitive advantage ... Achieving competitive advantage requires a firm to make a choice ... Being 'all things to all people' is a recipe for strategic mediocrity and below-average performance, because it often means that a firm has no competitive advantage at all". Porter suggested that it could be possible for a firm to achieve both cost leadership and differentiation, but only where its competitors are stuck in the middle, cost is greatly affected by market share or firm interrelationships, or a firm pioneers a major innovation[3]. All of these advantages could however be copied by competitors or eroded by industry change so were only temporary, at which point a firm needs to make a choice: "A firm should always aggressively pursue all cost reduction opportunities that do not sacrifice differentiation. A firm should also pursue all differentiation opportunities that are not costly. Beyond this point, however, a firm should be prepared to choose what its ultimate competitive advantage will be and resolve the trade-offs accordingly"[4].

Research during the 1980s generally supported Porter's position that a clear choice of generic strategies leads to superior performance, especially if that choice is associated with appropriate organization structures, and fits with the features of the competitive environment[5]. This research, however, also showed that firms could potentially combine some features of differentiation and cost leadership strategies, and that these strategies were not necessarily as distinct as Porter had argued. In this vein, it was argued for example that higher market share based on differentiation expenditure could lead to higher production volumes and therefore lower long run average costs; resulting in a combined strategy of differentiation and low cost[6].

A perception of mutual exclusivity of these strategies has gradually become strategic orthodoxy. At the time that Michael Porter developed and popularized his ideas on generic strategies in the late 1970s and early 1980s, the proposition that they were mutually exclusive was both reasonable and valid. Since then, however, things have changed. New organizational forms emerged that include outsourcing, virtual organizations and co-opetition. So have new working practices such as online, flexible and portfolio working; and new manufacturing technologies such as mass customization, as well as information technologies that break conventional trade-offs between richness and reach of communications. These developments, together with courageous, far-sighted leaders who conceive of better ways to organize and are prepared to stand apart from the herd and challenge conventional industry norms, have enabled a select few companies to break the trade-offs associated with these strategies and achieve the holy grail of strategy.

The Possibility of Janus Strategy

The idea that companies could balance features that are considered contradictory, incompatible or in tension has over time gained momentum. For example, professors Tushman and O'Reilly suggested[7] that companies should balance efficiency in the present with capacity-building for the future by creating separate, innovation-oriented subsidiaries within the corporate umbrella, that have their own strategies, tasks, competencies, cultures, structures, control systems and leadership styles. They called this institution of innovation subsidiaries separated from the parent "structural ambidexterity". The idea is that these subsidiaries would be co-ordinated with the parent company and other subsidiaries, and their outputs and innovations integrated with the main operations, by the senior executive team at the corporate level. This senior team would itself need to have ambidextrous thinking or paradoxical cognition[8] so that they could simultaneously hold competing ideas in their mind. As the case of Xerox and PARC that we will examine later shows, such an approach has significant challenges, including that the mindset of leaders is often not conducive to such a feat[9]. Structural ambidexterity also advocates however that business units that have different strategies, goals and capabilities should be separated; whereas Janus strategy supports the integration of potentially contradictory strategies and capabilities within a single operation such as for example in Narayana Health or Singapore Airlines.

Related research[10] has examined how companies can compete with dual business models, and also recommended that if there are serious potential conflicts between the models, the strategies should be kept separate in different subsidiaries. The assumption here is therefore that these business models would be found within different businesses with different brand identities within an overall corporate umbrella, rather than in a single business adopting a dual strategy. In case the markets these business models serve are similar however, the subsidiaries could be gradually integrated within the same overall organization to gain operational synergies.

Another approach is to focus on either horn of the dilemma sequentially, in what may be called temporal ambidexterity[11]. Of course, the other side of the dilemma cannot be forgotten, but patterns in the strategic actions of organizations[12] show that for several years they may focus on exploitation-oriented goals (such as corporate down-scoping, rationalization, pursuit of lean practices), and for other years they may focus on exploration-oriented goals (such as product or service innovation, cross-divisional transfer of learning, opening up new markets).

GE's corporate history offers an example of such a temporal solution[13]. The initial years of Jack Welch's corporate tenure between 1981 to 2001 were focused on exploitation and optimization goals. The aim was to simplify GE's corporate scope and focus the company on markets where it could lead. Corporate managers were tasked with being number one or number two in their markets. If they could not, the options were to fix, sell or close the business. In the late 1980s a program labeled "work-out" was initiated, with the goal of removing bureaucracy and instilling a culture of "speed, simplicity and self-confidence".

Then a phase focusing on exploration, learning and development began with a competitor benchmarking program labeled "best practices" and a program called "redefining leadership" that involved 360-degree assessment, management development, and a combined focus on performance and exhibiting company values. Then in the early 1990s GE focused on "boundaryless behavior" which focused on removing obstacles to the spreading of good ideas and learning through the company. In the mid-1990s GE shifted its focus from manufacturing to service businesses. In a return to an exploitation and optimization focus, the company then pursued Six Sigma Quality, a process that involved definition, measurement, analysis, improvement and control of quality. In the late 1990s the company sought leaders that could be "A" players with "4 Es"; energy, ability to energise others, competitive edge, and execution.

An ecological, network-based ambidexterity solution has also been proposed[14]. If companies can learn effectively from their networks, and also use make or buy decisions wisely to focus on doing what they can be best at while buying in for as low a price as possible the products and services they need, they can advance both efficiency and innovation goals.

When it comes to the role of individuals, research[15] has focused on softer issues such as the need to build competencies that can enable individuals balance competing goals in their everyday work, within a supportive organizational context. This model involves posing stretching performance targets coupled by social support, to enable individuals to balance alignment in the present with adaptability for the future. One challenge however is that a single framing of competing pressures (such as "we need to accomplish both innovation and efficiency") can be interpreted in radically different ways at different levels in the organization, and lead to different actions in terms of individuals' attempts to deal with these pressures[16].

Paths to ambidexterity	How	Why
Structural solution	Set up separate innovation subsidiaries with their own resources, culture and processes, to be coordinated by top management team	These subsidiaries can focus on innovation unaffected by bureaucracy of dominant organization
Temporal solution	Focus on either efficiency-exploitation or innovation-exploration goals at the corporate level, sequentially over time	It is easier to focus on one horn of the dilemma at a time, by segregating rather than transcending competing demands
Ecological solution	Create networks and partner with others with complementary capabilities. Gain synergies and learning through joint projects	Value is developed in ecosystems rather than in stand-alone entities. No single organization has all the necessary knowledge
Individual solution	Develop values and processes that empower individuals to make their own decisions about how to balance conflicting demands	Individuals and processes, rather than structures, is where balancing of competing demands takes place

Table 3.1. Paths to ambidexterity

Table 3.1 summarizes these main approaches[17]. Even though this body of research is enlightening, its prescriptions are often rather broad and high in the ladder of abstraction[18]. Further, a lot of research on ambidexterity has been conducted using cross-sectional, quantitative data from large samples of organizations. While this is an apt way to conduct research when testing hypotheses, it is not always useful when seeking to gain holistic, contextually informed insights. These are exactly the types of insights that are needed when we try to understand how a challenging pursuit such as Janus strategy can be realized. We can gain such insights if we investigate in some depth organizations that have accomplished this type of strategy, and try to distil the relevant principles or elements that can cut across individual organizations.

Having said that, this book is not a how-to manual. Pioneering strategies cannot be conceived and realized through following any number of set steps. This would be a contradiction in terms. No matter what classical, rationalist strategy approaches would have us believe, strategizing is a generative, creative endeavor. Organizations are less like machines and more like complex adaptive systems[19]. Sensemaking, storytelling, imagining, dreaming, showing the way ahead, appreciating and leveraging systemic connections, are as important as rational calculations; or even more so. The six elements below are part of the multi-color palette that strategists can draw on to create their masterpiece.

The Six Elements

The central message of this book is that companies do not have to be constrained by the trade-offs embedded in traditional, either/or strategic thinking. It is possible to achieve such things as effective innovation and high quality at low cost; gain the benefits of scale and size while maintaining agility; or make a global impact with lean resources.

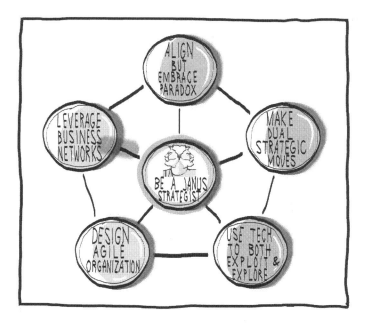

Figure 3.1. The six elements

My research in organizations that have accomplished such feats suggests six organizing principles that can enable an organization to implement Janus strategy. These principles are interconnected, working together as a system. Strategic moves within one domain shape others, and the strategist must have a deep appreciation of these systemic effects[20].

First, an organization must address any significant misalignments but at the same time it must embrace and grapple with the inevitable tensions, contradictions and paradoxes embedded in organizations. Strategic alignment is the base-level fitness that is needed for a company to survive the competitive game. Yet, high levels of alignment without experimentation and exploration can over time become dysfunctional, as we see in the chapters on Xerox and its Palo Alto Research Center (PARC). We discuss how organizations such as Toyota and Singapore Airlines have aligned but also embraced contradictions and paradoxes to gain competitive advantage.

Second, Janus strategists orchestrate the six elements; including themselves, since it takes conscious effort to develop oneself and others along these lines. Such development entails consciously committing to the search for synergistic solutions to strategic challenges that go beyond accepted wisdom or convention; the ability to simultaneously hold competing ideas in our mind; and building a paradoxical mindset, the ability to conceptualize challenges in terms of both/and, holistic rather than either/or binary terms[21]. Janus strategists are comfortable with contradictions and ambiguity (or at least willing to try to be), since many strategic challenges are by nature paradoxical and ambiguous. We expand on these issues in the final chapter.

Third, a company must make far-sighted, dual, synergistic strategic moves that are not simply based on short term return on investment calculations but mostly on the impact of such moves on both sides of a dilemma. Focusing on short and medium-term financials may be necessary, but it does not take into account strategic wisdom and foresight and may scupper investments that could otherwise prove exceptional and synergistic in the longer term. Apple's ongoing acquisition program for example focuses on technologies that the company will need for its product development such as artificial intelligence, healthcare, mapping and augmented reality[22]. These are relatively small acquisitions given Apple's size, and they provide needed technologies faster and at lower cost than if the company was to invent these itself.

Fourth, a company must make use of technology ambidextrously to both optimize, automate or increase efficiency, but also to simultaneously enhance quality, service levels, and innovation. To continue the example of Apple, its use of the same operating system (from more complex to simpler versions) across its devices is an example of ambidextrous use of technology. Average costs of operating system maintenance and development are reduced, and user experience is simultaneously enhanced due to easier inter-operatibility. An important strategic side-effect is strengthening the Apple ecosystem's pull, mitigating customers' bargaining power, and strengthening the company's market power[23]. We expand on Apple's Janus strategy in a subsequent chapter.

Fifth, the organization design must be conducive to such an enterprise; it must be both lean and simultaneously foster adaptability[24] and innovation. In other words, it must be agile, even at high scale. Accomplishing this feat necessitates strategic, leadership and organizational agility[25]. None of these dimensions is sufficient by itself; they are complementary and work together like a puzzle. We expand on these aspects of agility in the chapters on NASA.

Finally, in an interconnected world an organization must make the most of business networks and systems to develop and learn, as well as to optimize. We discuss for example NASA's development of its business model over the years towards the commercial network model, from its initial hierarchical and subsequently its inter-governmental partnership model[26]. In the network model the agency works with the commercial space sector and with private enterprise more broadly to seed, guide and access the frontier technologies it needs at lower cost than if it had to invent these itself.

Janus' Revenge: Playing with Fire

There are risks in attempting to synergise conventionally competing elements. Without the proper perspective, instead of achieving successful synergies, managers may over-emphasize one dimension, or even take ill-advised actions that lead to the loss of any previous workable balance and to risky failure. When James McNerney, a former GE executive became CEO at 3M in 2000, he decided to implement a Six Sigma program to streamline processes and increase efficiency. When this program was applied to 3M's heretofore effective research and development processes however it was a step too far. There is a difference between optimizing regular operational processes; and trying to optimize the more organic process of creativity, where innovation may not flourish if the climate is not conducive. Six Sigma involves documentation, reporting and streamlining, whereas research and development involves experimentation, search, inspiration and happenstance. Predictably, 3M's innovation waned over the next few years, and a new CEO appointed in 2005, George Buckley, wisely decided to exempt 3M's research and development processes from Six Sigma. According to Buckley: "Invention is by its very nature a disorderly process.... You can't put a Six Sigma process into that area and say, well, I'm getting behind on invention, so I'm going to schedule myself for three good ideas on Wednesday and two on Friday. That's not how creativity works"[27]. The dampening of innovation at 3M due to the implementation of Six Sigma in its research and development processes was part of a broader trend of corporations jumping on the bandwagon of optimization. Out of a sample of 58 corporations that implemented Six Sigma, 91% had lower growth subsequently as compared to the S&P 500[28].

Schlitz beer is another case in point, where efforts to achieve higher efficiency while trying to sustain quality ultimately destroyed the company[29]. The Joseph Schlitz Brewing Company was incorporated in 1858, having acquired a brewery founded by August Krug in 1849. Schlitz's revenues grew quickly, becoming the best selling beer in the United States in 1902, subsequently competing with Annheuser-Busch for the top spot over the next half century. In 1976 Schlitz was still the second best-selling beer in America. In the early 1970s however, senior management decided that they wanted to raise profitability by lowering the cost of production of the flagship brand of the brewery, Schlitz beer. They decided to replace some of the malted barley with cheaper corn syrup, added a silica gel to prevent the formation of haze in the beer, used high-temperature fermentation which took less time than the traditional fermentation method, and replaced some of the other ingredients with cheaper extracts.

The result was a beer that did not taste at all like the original, and did not keep as long. In 1976, amid concerns that the Food and Drug Administration would require disclosure of production ingredients including the silica gel, the gel was replaced with a chemical called "Chill-garde" that would be filtered out before the beer was distributed, and would therefore be non-disclosable. This chemical however did not react well with the foam stabilizer also being used in the production process, and small white flakes begun to form in the beer. After months of denying or downplaying the issue, Schlitz was forced to recall 10 million bottles. The reputation of the company suffered, and market share dived. This was followed by marketing campaigns that were perceived as rather aggressive by customers and hurt Schlitz's reputation even more. A large strike by production employees in June 1981 was the final straw. Schlitz was subsequently acquired by Stroh in 1982, which was itself acquired by Pabst in 1999. Pabst then set forth to recreate Schlitz's classic flavor through research on historical company documents and interviews of former brew-masters and taste-testers. The classic Schlitz beer was then re-introduced; yet the Schlitz brand is now a shadow of its former self. Schlitz is a cautionary tale of what could happen when the delicate juggling act between competing goals (in this case product quality and cost) goes astray amid misguided decisions that seek to increase performance but may end up hurting the company.

Schroedinger's cat leading the army. Or, "align but
embrace paradox"

4

Align but Embrace Paradox

S trategic alignment is the base-level fitness that is necessary before an organization can embark on the more challenging pursuit of Janus Strategy. Alignment exists when a firm's strategy is appropriate given the demands of the competitive environment, and the constraints and opportunities that it affords (external alignment); and when the firm's organization design and competencies support and effectively operationalize its strategy (internal alignment). One way to map and diagnose the strategic alignment of an organization is the ESCO model. This stands for Environment (at the competitive, macro-economic and institutional dimensions), Strategy of the company (at the business, corporate or global levels depending on the purposes of the analysis), Competencies supporting the strategy, and Organization that operationalizes the strategy; the functions and processes that should work in an integrated manner to deliver these core competencies.

This process needs to be driven and orchestrated by Leadership which does not only refer to senior management, but leaders at every level of the organization. Finally, if the firm is internally and externally aligned, there are higher chances of achieving competitive advantage[1].

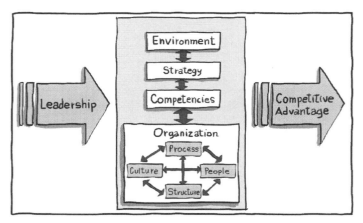

Figure 4.1. The ESCO model of strategic alignment

ESCO helps strategists ask the right questions: Given what is happening in our environment, do we have the right strategy? If not, how does it need to change? Could we shape our environment in some way? Do we have the right core competencies to support our current and intended strategy? Are our operations configured to deliver the competencies we need in an integrated, mutually supportive manner? Finally, where are the key misalignments and what can we do about them? These questions are inevitably hard to answer, and involve debate, difficult choices, uncomfortable evaluations and political battles. But there is no alternative than to ask and address them. Otherwise inertia, personal agendas and even happenstance could be allowed to play dangerously influential roles. Strategic alignment is a continuously moving target, and misalignments can creep in at any point.

External Misalignment

External misalignment occurs when the strategy is out of sync with the competitive environment. One example of such a misalignment occurred when many western brewing giants rushed into the Chinese beer market in the mid-1990s, collectively investing billions of dollars in building state of the art factories. Following a generic strategy of differentiation, they produced premium beer sold under their global brand names for around five times the price of locally branded beer, that sold as cheaply as soft drinks. However, they painfully discovered that the premium segment of the beer market was limited to only around 5% of total demand, consumers were fiercely loyal to their local brands, local competitors were quick to engage in predatory price competition, the weak transport infrastructure made it harder to transport beer to other regions economically, and local bureaucrats were not always transparent or easy to deal with.

While these premium, global competitors had high levels of internal alignment (their operations and competencies were aligned with their strategy), there was a critical external misalignment between their strategy and the competitive environment. Their premium offerings were not consistent with what the bulk of the market wanted or could afford (cheap, good enough beer), were at odds with key aspects of the environment (inadequate infrastructure and unpredictable bureaucracy). The outcome was that most of these new global entrants were unable to keep sustaining huge losses year after year and had to exit the Chinese market after selling their state-of-the-art factories to local competitors such as Tsing Tao at bargain basement prices[2].

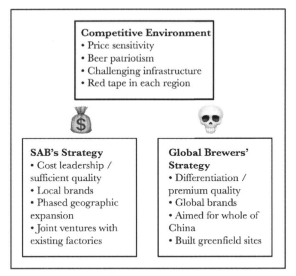

Figure 4.2. SAB's vs global brewers' China entry strategy

However, South African Breweries (now SAB Miller) succeeded in China by adopting a different strategy: a cost leadership, regional strategy that was aligned with the demands of the competitive environment (external alignment). SAB gave high priority to strategic alliances as a means of gaining local knowledge, becoming a part of local networks and building a deep understanding of local consumer behavior. This enabled SAB to keep its sunk costs manageable by not building brand new factories but investing to upgrade its local partners' existing factories. Further, SAB realized that rather than offer globally branded beer at premium prices, the market at that point would best support local brands at local prices; and that a fast, China-wide geographic expansion strategy was not realistic at the time. It therefore pursued phased, gradual expansion based on regional strongholds. SAB got it right largely because it already had experience of competing effectively in emerging markets. It been able to learn from operating in places such as such as sub-Saharan Africa and Eastern Europe, environments that posed many similar challenges, and could then effectively transfer that learning to its China operations. Over the next ten to fifteen years, as the beer market gradually matured in China, the premium segment grew enough to support differentiation strategies. Most global brewers had implemented differentiation ahead of its time in the early 1990s and paid dearly for it. The figure below compares SAB's China market entry strategy with other global brewers' strategies in the context of important environmental features.

Internal Misalignment

Operational configurations and processes can be mutually inconsistent in their orientations and goals. This can occur at the functional, cross-divisional or corporate levels. One classic and widespread form of misalignment is "the folly of rewarding A while hoping for B[3]". In academia for example, one receives the rewards that matter to most professors, such as tenure or a full professorship in a world class university mainly for one thing; research quality and productivity as evidenced in high-level journal publications. Yet, great teaching and earnest performance in administrative and pastoral duties are also hoped for. Further, some companies reward employees based on quantifiable measures of individual performance such as sales figures, yet hope for a teamwork culture and sharing of customer information and leads. Some firms reward managers based on quarterly financial performance of their department or division, yet hope that these same managers work to create a climate where customers receive a great experience in their use of the service and in their interactions with the company. Great customer experience and financial performance ideally go together as part of a desirable virtuous circle; but focusing on one part of a desirable whole can lead to distortions in emphasis that undermine the other parts.

Often a company has a stated strategy for which it has not developed the right competencies and for which it is not properly organized. For example, a European firm in the telecom sector instituted a successful marketing program and cool, youthful positioning strategy that helped the company achieve double-digit growth over the next few years. Yet, its customer care capability had not developed accordingly to handle the higher volume of customers. When customers called the company they were made to wait on the line for long periods of time, causing tensions and dissatisfaction, with the potential to impact adversely the firm's market positioning and jeopardize further growth. The company realized this and took steps to address the deficiencies in its customer care function and align it with its market positioning.

At the corporate level, the historical challenges of achieving rapid development and global roll-out of innovations in multinational giants such as Procter and Gamble indicate less than ideal levels of cross-divisional alignment[4]. P&G's mode of global expansion after the setting up of its overseas division in 1948 involved extensive duplication of operations and processes in several new markets, in effect creating smaller P&G clones in each market, with high levels of operational independence. This led to low levels of cross-national co-ordination on processes such as new product development, lower efficiency, development of a "not invented here" syndrome, and fierce independence of international operations. In the 1980's there were concerted efforts to address these issues through increasing cross-national integration and co-ordination of key functions. By the 1990's the international division was replaced by four regional organizations structured through a matrix (regions / product categories), that included global category executives; but innovation and diffusion were still too slow. This prompted a further change program initiated in 1998 labeled "Organization 2005", seen as the most fundamental and dramatic change in P&G's history. This was a corporate restructuring program that involved the creation of seven product-based global business units, supported by "market development organizations" as well as global business services to centralize support functions.

The company still did not achieve the levels of growth and innovation it expected despite a series of restructurings over the years[5]. Historically, the organizational culture and corporate design of P&G led to less than ideal levels of cross-divisional and cross-national alignment, that among other things impacted the innovation and global rollout of new products. Alignment efforts for complex, multi-divisional, global organizations such as P&G are necessarily a work in progress.

Failure to Re-align in the Face of Environmental Change

A company may have a highly aligned model across the four ESCO elements at a particular point, but its leaders may not monitor changes in the external environment or evaluate their impact. Tight strategic alignment and focus on a particular business model or competency brings with it the risk of inertia and rigidity, especially if the culture does not encourage vigorous debate or constructive dissent[6]. Such cultures may be hostile to diversity, suffer from groupthink, dwell on history and past successes, tolerate unproductive politics, or characterized by a sense of invincibility that leads to complacency[7].

One company that did not effectively adapt to environmental change is Wang Laboratories, founded in 1951, once the leader in network enterprise computing. Wang did not appreciate the extent to which the arrival of the personal computer would encroach on its market. Executives did not realize that it would in fact be cheaper for many companies to buy several personal computers for their employees rather than Wang's more expensive mainframe-based system that also tied clients to Wang in terms of regular maintenance costs. There was also lack of compatibility of Wang computers with other available software because of Wang's proprietary standards. Certain senior appointments in the company led to several senior managers leaving the company in protest.

In 1990 the company undertook significant restructuring and started focusing more on software than hardware, but the move was too late; it filed for bankruptcy in 1992[8].

Kodak is another case in point. The first digital camera was invented by Steven Sasson, a 24-year-old Kodak employee in 1975, two years after he joined the company. When he demonstrated it to executives, they were underwhelmed. Sasson recalls: "They were convinced that no one would ever want to look at their pictures on a television set ... Print had been with us for over 100 years, no one was complaining about prints, they were very inexpensive, and so why would anyone want to look at their picture on a television set[9]?" Kodak executives did not want to cannibalize the goose that laid the golden eggs, their film and printing business. "My prototype was big as a toaster, but the technical people loved it ... But it was filmless photography, so management's reaction was, 'that's cute - but don't tell anyone about it'[10]."

Kodak's lucrative business model encompassed every stage of the process, including Kodak film, flash cubes, processing, and paper. Kodak patented the first digital camera in 1978. In 1989 Sasson developed a prototype single lens reflex (S.L.R.) camera with a 1.2 megapixel sensor, with image compression and memory card, that was not introduced to market. When competitors introduced digital cameras, Kodak earned billions in royalty payments from manufacturers who used its technology, until its patent expired in 2007. At that point Kodak introduced its own digital camera, around two decades after Japanese competitors did so. This got off to a good start, with US market share of 16.6% in 2008, that nevertheless slid to 11.6% by 2011 as competition from lower cost producers intensified[11]. After efforts to restructure, Kodak filed for bankruptcy protection in January 2012, also announcing that it would exit the digital camera business. Between 2003 and 2012 the company had fired 47,000 employees, entering bankruptcy protection with the remaining 17,000 employees. At its height, the company had 145,000 employees[12]. The restructuring process had cost $3.4bn, and through it Kodak shed $4.1bn of debt. The company emerged from bankruptcy protection in August 2013 as a shadow of its former self with 8,500 employees. It focused on printing technology for corporate customers, touch-screen components for smartphones and tablets, and film for the movie industry[13]. By that time the company had exited the consumer photography market that it had pioneered. Kodak continued to shrink; by 2020 the company had around 5,000 employees.

A company that managed to realign successfully on the other hand is IBM. Under Gerstner's leadership, realizing that most segments involving hardware were gradually becoming commoditized and unattractive in terms of profit potential, the company gradually reduced its investments and operations in mass-market hardware manufacturing and increased its capabilities in high-end servers, software, services and consulting[14]. In doing so IBM realigned its strategy with environmental shifts and refocused on high-growth and high-return segments. Lou Gerstner took over in 1993, after IBM had lost US$16bn between 1991-93. He had initially refused the CEO job, concerned that he lacked the technological background to lead IBM. However, his decisions about the future of the company were based not on technological knowledge but on attention to market trends, the customer's perspective and judicious portfolio management. The customer's view is what led him for example to make a U-turn on a momentous plan to break up IBM into smaller businesses, since for a customer it was easier and more effective to buy technology from an integrator rather than from several different suppliers. Gerstner strove to change IBM's culture from an inward-directed, politically charged one where divisions were behaving like fiefdoms, to a customer-focused, integrated one with a corporate-wide outlook. He pursued open technology standards and led a focus on services rather than hardware. More recently the company continued its adaptation with a focus on cloud and artificial intelligence-based services[15].

The Inevitability of Paradox

Even though alignment is far from easy to achieve, leading companies exhibit effective strategic alignment that they can sustain over time through being adaptable in the face of industry shifts, competitor actions, changing customer demands, and their own strategy and operations. This process is paradoxical, involving simultaneous stability and change; simultaneous alignment and adaptation. Paradoxes specific to leadership behaviors include maintaining humility while at the same time having a robust sense of self; and being able to maintain control while letting go of control at the same time[16].

Paradoxes are part and parcel of organizational life. As the CEO of W. L. Gore & Associates put it, "We have a few paradoxes that we continually try to manage. One is striking the balance between meeting short-term and long-term objectives. Another one is creating the right focus on innovation and at the same time driving improvements in efficiency and effectiveness. A third one is balancing what we call the 'power of our small team' with the greater needs of the enterprise. These are all tensions we try to balance on a daily basis.[17]" There is a multitude of paradoxes that are endemic in every organization. These include for example achieving both empowerment and control, diversity and homogeneity, global synergies and local adaptation[18].

The very idea of strategy is itself paradoxical, in the sense that strategy should be both stable as well as changeable. It should both provide clear, unified direction, we well as allow for frequent maneuvering on demand. To deal with this paradox, companies tackle different strategy dimensions in different ways. Values that define how the company should do business such as high levels of customer orientation, global aspects of a brand, or important aspects of brand identity need to be relatively stable. Simultaneously, companies may gradually change their strategy by taking particular actions in the context of the broader values, such as market entry or exit or corporate portfolio shifts[19].

Yet, paradoxes are generative because they can spur the search for both/and solutions that transcend binary, either/or logic. As Arthur Koestler noted during his exploration of creativity, "comic discovery is paradox stated-scientific discovery is paradox resolved"[20]. In other words, we find jokes funny because of the unexpected conjunction of two domains that are normally distinct. When two seemingly unrelated domains are brought together in science, such as electricity and magnetism that had been considered separate until the 1820s, such a conjunction addresses long standing challenges and creates a new field; in this case electromagnetism. Paradoxical thinking is consistent with the nature of the challenges strategists have to deal with, since strategic problems often involve contradictory dimensions. In order to combat the inertia and conservatism that build up over time, partly as a consequence of the pursuit of alignment, we need the generative power of paradoxes[21].

Embracing Contradictions and Paradoxes at Toyota

Toyota's success as a leading global competitor in mobility has been attributed to how the company embeds paradoxes in its functioning[22]. As researchers on Toyota note, "studies of human cognition show that when people grapple with opposing insights, they understand the different aspects of an issue and come up with effective solutions. So Toyota deliberately fosters contradictory viewpoints within the organization and challenges employees to find solutions by transcending differences rather than resorting to compromises. This culture of tensions generates innovative ideas that Toyota implements to pull ahead of competitors, both incrementally and radically[23]". The authors identify six main contradictions: Toyota moves slowly yet also takes big leaps; it grows and performs well but is also paranoid about its success; it is extremely efficient but employees seemingly waste time on things such as attending unnecessary meetings; it is both frugal but also spends lavishly on some aspects of its operations; its internal communications are simple yet based on complex social networks; and finally it has a hierarchical culture, yet employees have freedom to disagree and challenge senior people.

A separate study of Toyota's NUMMI plant in California[24] revealed key organizational mechanisms through which Toyota managed to grapple with the paradox of accomplishing both efficiency and flexibility, rather than accepting that more efficiency (via standardization of operations) necessarily means less flexibility, and vice versa. This plant performed well above industry average on measures of both efficiency and flexibility. The researchers found that Toyota accomplished flexibility through four mechanisms: using metaroutines (having standard procedures for changing existing routines to new ones); enrichment (mixing routine tasks with non-routine tasks); switching (separating routine from non-routine tasks by focusing on them at different times and moving employees between these tasks); and partitioning (creating subunits that temporarily focus on routine or non-routine tasks). In this way, NUMMI managed to deal with challenges such as model changeovers smoothly, without sacrificing efficiency.

Grappling with paradoxes is embedded in Toyota's values and operations. According to former CEO Katsuaki Watanabe "people can use revolutionary approaches while making incremental improvements. The two have different focuses; there's continuous change in Kaizen and discontinuous change in kakushin.

I am only trying to get people to make the leap from incremental improvement to radical improvement whenever possible[25]".

Underlying the organizational improvements and innovations brought about by the generative power of paradox are the Toyota Guiding Principles that shape its global operations (such as respect other cultures and customs), business values (such as providing clean and safe products), corporate culture (such as valuing both the individual and the team), and partnerships (creating long term alliances to achieve mutual benefits[26]).

Toyota's effectiveness involves both "hard" elements such as its lean production system, and "soft" elements, such as its culture of using contradictions in a generative manner. Synergizing hard and soft elements is an idea with ancient origins, for example the Yin and Yang found in Chinese philosophy. Yin and yang are not merely opposites. Rather, they are complementary; they interpenetrate and they are synergistic, producing something bigger than the sum of their parts. Their interrelationship creates the Tao, or the Way.

The Boston Consulting Group recommended as one option that "firms should consider separating exploratory business units from exploitative core activities and giving them differentiated 'performance contracts' with tailored goals, metrics, and incentives[27]." This is essentially a prompt for "structural ambidexterity[28]." Such an approach can enable innovative subsidiaries to function and grow without being suffocated by the structures and values of the main business that may be incompatible with a different business model. While such a separation approach may be appropriate for many organizations, it is still not Janus Strategy as we have defined it, because it separates opposing forces and houses them in different parts of the business rather than holding them in generative tension in the same part of the business, as in the case of Toyota, Narayana Health, or as we will see in the next chapter, Singapore Airlines.

Heraclitus of Ephesus pondering one of the earliest
renditions of paradoxes in the fifth century BC. We cannot
step into the same river twice since the water is always
flowing so it's not the same river, and we are not the same
person across time. Yet the river is still there, and it is in
many ways the same river; and we are also in many ways the
same person. Heraclitus is also making one of the first
arguments for the constitutive nature of process; that is,
everything, including reality, is in a constant state of flux

5

Alignment and Paradoxes at Singapore Airlines

Singapore Airlines (SIA) has become one of the highest performing and respected airlines in the world through its ability to offer consistent service excellence combined with intense efficiency levels. In addition to numerous service awards, 2020 was the 25th year that SIA was voted "best international airline"[1]. In terms of generic strategies, this is an integration of cost leadership and differentiation, something that Harvard Professor Michael Porter, the originator of generic strategies, argued was not sustainable in the longer term[2]. In his line of argument, these different strategies involve different types of investments, alignments, internal processes and market positioning and are therefore incompatible. Trying to implement both of them would lead to internal conflicts and confusion. Professor Porter maintained that such a combination would be impossible to maintain in the long run, and that organizations that attempted it would end up "stuck in the middle" and lose any competitive advantage they previously had. These observations were made on a solid basis in the 1980s, but since then things have changed. New technologies, organization designs and forms of employment create options for organizations that enable the transcendence or re-framing of trade-offs. Empirical observation shows that some outstanding companies can accomplish integrated strategies, as outlined in this book.

Singapore Airlines for example has successfully synergized these potentially competing strategies for decades through mastering paradox[3]. We explore how the airline addresses both poles of paradoxes, an ambidextrous capability that enables the realization of the Janus strategy of cost leadership combined with differentiation[4] and affords competitive advantage. Specifically, SIA's strategy implementation centers around four paradoxes: cost effective service excellence[5], simultaneous decentralized and centralized innovation, being simultaneously a follower and a leader in service development, and accomplishing standardization as well as personalization in customer interactions.

SIA's balance sheet has almost no gearing and the airline has funded its growth largely through retained earnings while still consistently paying dividends. SIA has outperformed the industry throughout most of its history, delivering healthy returns since its founding in 1972. It reported an annual loss in 2012 after taking an impairment charge when disposing its stake in Virgin airlines, and has reported profitability broadly equivalent to the industry during 2015-17. Other than that, its profitability has been consistently above the industry since its founding in 1972[6].

Figure 5.1. Singapore Airlines' net profit margin vs industry

Given the focus of this chart on the last two decades, and the lower margins between SIA's and industry performance over the last few years, one might wonder whether Singapore Airlines has been losing its competitive advantage. There has been relentless imitation of innovations that Singapore Airlines had introduced over the years; and the competitive intensity of the industry has increased. Singapore Airlines initiated a transformational change program in 2017 with the aim to help the airline reclaim its market leadership. This program focused on three domains[7] including "leveraging digital" that encompasses agile methodologies[8]. The "digital innovation blueprint" that is part of this program supports the airline's ambition to "be the leading digital airline in the world. We want to offer the best customer experience, whether it is through digital, on-board, or on-ground. We want to optimize operations so we can be efficient and cost-effective. We also want to enable our employees to be productive and leverage innovation to generate new business revenue and opportunities[9]".

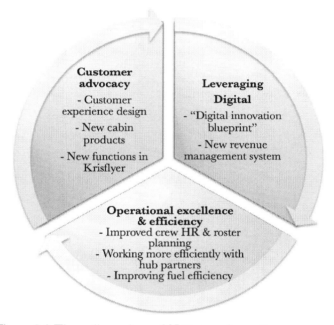

Figure 5.2 Three dimensions of SIA's transformation program

Future years will indicate whether the gains of this program will translate into enhanced competitive advantage and performance. What is beyond doubt is that over the last five decades, the airline posted an annual loss only once, and surpassed industry net profit performance in all other years expect two, when it was almost equal to that performance. This is an exceptional long-term record.

SIA's performance over the decades has been accomplished in the context of an unforgiving, hypercompetitive industry environment. Globally, the industry has never earned a real rate of return on its capital employed[10], and has in fact destroyed shareholder value like few other industries. The covid-19 pandemic of early 2020 has further devastated industry returns. In June 2020 the International Air Transport Association (IATA) forecasted that the net profit margins of the industry would reduce from 3.1% in 2019 to negative 20.1 in 2020; the global aircraft fleet would shrink by a third from around 30,000 airplanes to around 20,000, and employment in the industry would also shrink by around a third, from 2.9 million individuals to 1.87 million[11]. Comparative performance across airlines will be available when the dust settles, annual reports encompassing the effects of this devastating period are published.

Embracing Paradox

A paradox perspective can offer insights into how Singapore Airlines can operationalize Janus strategy through apparently contradictory organizational capabilities. Seeking to synthesize opposing poles of paradoxes[12] encourages thinking in terms of both/and dualities, rather than in terms of either/or dualisms. SIA's paradoxes are shown in Table 5.1 below.

SIA's paradoxes	Low cost (internal efficiency) through	Differentiation (externally) through
Paradox 1	Cost effective...	service excellence
Paradox 2	Simultaneous de-centralized and...	centralized innovation
Paradox 3	Being a follower...	as well as a leader in service development
Paradox 4	Standardization, as well as...	personalization in customer interactions

Table 5.1. Four paradoxes at Singapore Airlines

These competing combinations occur at both the levels of strategy as well as organization, where strategy is realized. In terms of strategy, SIA has achieved both sustained differentiation through innovation and service excellence, as well as cost leadership in its peer group. SIA has been the most awarded airline in the world and has maintained a consistent five-star record on the Skytrax service awards with just a handful of other global airlines[13]. At the same time, SIA has achieved cost leadership, something normally inconsistent with superior quality.

In the airline industry a common measure of cost is cents per available seat kilometer (ASK). This calculation includes all operating expenditure for a flight, such as salaries, fuel, depreciation, and catering (less cargo revenues for that flight) divided by available seat kilometers (number of available seats times number of kilometers flown). SIA's average cost per available seat kilometer during the period 2001-2009 was US$4.57 cents (Singapore $7.47 cents, using average exchange rates for this period), as shown by data in its Annual Reports. In the middle of this period, in 2005, full service airlines had ASK costs of between US$8 to 16 cents in Europe, 7 to 8 cents in the US, and 5 to 7 cents in Asia. Budget carriers had costs of between 4 to 8 cents in Europe, 5 to 6 cents in the US and 2 to 3 cents in Asia[14]. Further, a 2016 study confirmed that Singapore Airlines had one of the lowest cost levels compared to other Asia-Pacific and global full-service peer airlines[15].

SIA Paradox 1: Achieving Cost Effective Service Excellence

Usually service excellence at all touchpoints of the customer experience involves comparatively higher costs, and vice versa. At SIA high quality and low cost are not seen as contradictory however. The airline engages in strategic human resource management processes[16] such as extensive training that lasts for four and a half months, more than twice as long as the industry average. Training includes unusual topics such as wine appreciation, interaction style and poise, and emotional and cultural intelligence. This investment in training supports service excellence, which increases customer loyalty and reduces turnover of customers, therefore reducing customer acquisition costs. The curriculum includes an understanding of the airline industry and its economics, inculcating to all new recruits the understanding that SIA has to continually control costs and find ways to do things more efficiently in order to survive, which creates sensitivity towards avoiding waste and reinforces the cultural value of frugality.

Further, there are ongoing programs such as SIA (Staff Ideas in Action)[17] that encourage employees to come forward with ideas for improving operations and service levels. SIA gives awards to recognise both contributors of ideas, and instances of excellent service of staff who go beyond the call of duty. There is empowerment of both young managers and frontline staff, giving the opportunity to gain exposure through high levels of responsibility. SIA encourages experimentation in terms of implementing new processes internally; so that by the time a new offering or process are experienced by the customer they must be seamless.

The policy of internal promotions (vs external appointments), leads to senior people who have in-depth understanding of the SIA way and can provide not only technical knowledge, but also political and emotional support to junior employees, and through the process instilling the company values to them. There is a management rotation system that encourages a broad, corporate outlook and a sense of common destiny rather than narrow perspectives and parochialism.

SIA's infrastructure strategy contributes to service excellence as well as efficiency. The airline has one of the youngest fleets in the world, with an average age of six years and seven months[18], compared to the industry average of around ten years in Asia Pacific, 11 years in Western Europe, and 14 years in North America[19]. A young fleet has lower repair and maintenance costs and lower fuel consumption. It can also support a higher aircraft utilization rate, reducing average costs in an asset-heavy industry. Changi Airport, SIA's hub, is regularly voted as the world's best airport, and is also one of the most efficient in terms of its charges to airlines.

With respect to employee productivity, a study[20] showed that SIA employees were the second most productive airline employees (in terms of available tonne/km per $1,000 of labor cost) after Korean Airlines. High employee productivity is due to a number of reasons. First, SIA is headquartered in Singapore where meritocracy is widely accepted and combined with a strong work ethic. Second, SIA through its brand can attract bright young graduates who are motivated to perform and learn. The combination of relatively conservative starting salaries with significant responsibilities given to these young graduates only a few months into their jobs helps them develop and enhances productivity. Third, SIA salaries are about average in the Singapore labor market, and lower compared to large European and US airlines. Staff accept the remuneration package because of the exposure and development they receive when working in SIA. They get to associate with a world leading company and have significant responsibility early on in their careers. If they leave SIA, they are highly sought after in other service industries.

SIA's employees take a keen interest in the airline's profitability and understand the importance of service excellence combined with cost effectiveness in achieving profitability. This interest is partly motivated though the bonus scheme, where all employees receive an annual bonus based on the same formula, directly related to profitability. The bonus could be up to half the salary when profitability is high, or zero during years of low profitability. The bonus scheme combined with pre-set, automatic salary cuts during downturns give employees a strong stake in the financial performance of SIA. This policy creates high alignment between performance and reward and helps to keep the cost structure flexible especially during downturns when preserving cash and cutting fixed costs matter most.

All these factors combined lead to a dual culture in SIA – anything that customers experience has to exude quality and be consistent with the airline's premium service positioning. Anything in the background is subjected to rigorous cost control. For example, SIA's headquarters is in a low cost location in an old aircraft hangar at Changi airport, and has very modest interiors. Symbolic messages such as this reinforce the cultural value of frugality and are visible reminders when dealing with suppliers and operating aircraft.

SIA Paradox 2: Simultaneous Centralized and Decentralized Innovation

SIA has a reputation of being a serial innovator, having introduced many firsts in the airline industry over the years, and having sustained this innovative orientation over decades in the face of intense cost pressures, industry crises, and trends towards commoditization[21]. Examples include SIA's Krisworld entertainment system, Dolby sound, book-the-cook service where flyers can order the dishes they want to eat in advance, and the widest business class seats in the world at the time when the A380 was introduced.

SIA's approach to innovation involves the combination of hard, structured, rigorous, and centralized innovation, as well as soft, emergent, distributed, decentralized innovation[22]. Based in the product innovation department, centralized innovations follow a structured process and involve steps such as opportunity identification and selection, concept evaluation, design and development, and launch. Ideas for major innovations may emerge from discussions with suppliers, feedback from customers, or proactive searching for ideas on the internet, at technology fairs or industry conferences.

The product innovation department consists of a small group of people who tend to rotate in and out from other departments around the organization every two to three years. For major projects such as the launch of a new type of plane with a revitalised product offering key team members may remain longer until the entire development cycle is carried out. The department's key task is to conceive several innovative ideas and move selected ones through the development cycle to commercial introduction. The core team is augmented by staff from all departments on shorter-term placements, to bring in specific knowledge. Conceiving new ideas and moving them through the cycle are the main key performance indicators for individuals in this department.

This hard, centralized approach is complemented by a softer, less structured emergent innovation process that may be labeled "distributed innovation". This is initiated and implemented by individual departments around the company rather than by the central product innovation department. Distributed innovations tend to focus on continuous improvement and incremental innovation rather than on radically new offerings. This process is funded by departmental budgets unless higher levels of investment are needed at a later stage. Distributed innovation is especially useful in ensuring that the totality of the components of a service encounter work well together and that functional departments focus on improving and aligning their respective services.

This distributed process reinforces the cultural value that innovation is everyone's concern at SIA, and is an ongoing process, rather than being something that a specialized department will take care of. Further, the influence and direct involvement of various facets of operations in the innovation process means that the ability to consistently deliver in service interactions, a cornerstone of SIA's success, is upheld by only introducing innovations that can be delivered reliably and smoothly. Further, these innovations have a dual focus; given the cost pressures in aviation, innovations should ideally bring about savings while at the same time achieving improvements in service quality.

The distributed innovation process is revitalised by rotating early-career executives across the company who are keen to make their mark and advance in the company. Managers in all roles are rotated except specialists in the finance, accounting, legal and engineering departments. In addition to creating opportunities for managers to prove themselves, rotation provides cultural integration across departments that might otherwise develop inward-looking subcultures.

SIA Paradox 3: Being a Leader and a Follower at the Same Time

Being both a leader and a follower at the same time but in different areas, enables the airline to both sustain service excellence and also control cost. The choice of where to lead or follow depends on what areas are seen as crucial for customer experience. SIA aims to be a leader and innovate in all processes that the customer experiences. Simultaneously, it is a conservative follower, engaging in incremental improvements using tried and tested technology in back-office functions that customers do not directly experience. This focus derives from SIA's historical decisions. In the early 1970s the airline created service offerings that were inconsistent with IATA rules that were too prescriptive at the time, which prompted SIA to temporarily leave IATA. These early innovations were simple but ended up significantly changing the travel experience when they were imitated over time by competitors. They included offering free alcoholic drinks on board, better quality food and free headphones to watch movies.

On the other hand, to reduce cost and implementation risk, SIA is a follower at the back office and other non-customer facing processes. For example, the airline implemented a revenue management system which was largely off the rack and had been successfully implemented in many other airlines. SIA's headquarters is located in Changi Airport in an old hangar rather than in a shiny new building in the centre of town. There are no luxuries such as a high end gym or expensive coffee machines in this building. The airline's focus is firmly where its customers and other stakeholders can experience it, creating competitive differentiation. In the back office the attention shifts from higher-risk, high-impact innovations to continuous improvement and cost effectiveness. Simultaneous innovation on many fronts is seen as too risky, and managers believe that SIA needs a stable, reliable operational base to enable it to offer both incremental and radical innovations to passengers.

SIA Paradox 4: Achieving Simultaneous Personalization and Standardization

Standardization relating to areas such as service procedures, internal processes, information technology systems and infrastructure leads to predictability, safety, and cost control. Where standardization supports customer facing processes it also leads to customer satisfaction. However, standardization cannot lead to consistent customer delight since customers will grow to expect a particular level of service. SIA's approach to delighting customers therefore relies on combining standardization with personalization. There is standardization of on-board service processes such as the way the cabin crew greet passengers and serve food and drinks. Whereas standardization supports customer satisfaction and consistent delivery of the service experience, personalization makes passengers feel special and individual because it is unexpected and not routine from the passenger's perspective.

Personalization is supported by an ingrained culture of customer service, developed historically and sustained by strategic human resource management processes including selection, recruitment, training, reward and evaluation, and technology investments. These processes instil pride and a strong sense of organizational identity. Examples of personalization include passengers at high tiers in the frequent flyer program being greeted by name or cabin crew knowing a frequent flyer's favorite wine or drink and bringing it to them even before they request it. Personalization can also be emergent, as for example when a passenger requests a vegetarian meal without having reserved it and without the flight menu containing a vegetarian option. The flight crew can creatively put together a vegetarian meal for that person from whatever food options are available on the flight. In addition to optimizing operations, the airline's "digital innovation blueprint" initiated in 2017 aims both to increase efficiency as well as to strengthen customer service through higher personalization. According to George Wang, Senior Vice President of IT at SIA "We don't just do digital for digital's sake. We do it with a focus on improving customer service"[23].

As noted at the beginning of this chapter, SIA's four paradoxes support an overall Janus strategy of integrated differentiation through service excellence, together with cost leadership. Differentiation is achieved via excellence in all processes that the customers experience, whereas cost leadership is achieved by reducing costs in back office operations, as well as via a number of particular functional choices as well as decisions relating to the six elements of Janus strategy. In the next chapter we delve deeper into how SIA realizes Janus strategy from these perspectives.

Singapore Airlines has been an archetype of Janus strategy since its inception. This is firstly in terms of its simultaneous objectives to offer service excellence through innovation, quality of infrastructure and customer interaction, and simultaneously doing so with exceptional efficiency. Secondly, as we have seen in this chapter, in its operations it manages fundamental paradoxes in a generative manner

6

Janus Strategy at Singapore Airlines

We saw in the previous chapter that Singapore Airlines' strategy combines internal cost leadership with external differentiation[1], and that the implementation of this strategy centers around four paradoxes[2]: cost effective service excellence[3], simultaneous decentralized and centralized innovation, being simultaneously a follower and a leader in service development, and accomplishing standardization as well as personalization in customer interactions.

Paradoxes however are just one lens through which to explore strategy realization and strategic thinking. In this chapter we expand on how Singapore Airlines implements Janus strategy through the lens of functional strategies such as marketing, human resource or operations strategies; through the lens of activity systems; through the ESCO alignment model; and finally, through the six elements of Janus strategy. There is no single silver bullet, no magic concept or framework that can give us all the answers. What we do have is multiple perspectives that can illuminate different aspects of multi-faceted challenges such as Janus strategy and how it may be realized.

Historical Development of SIA's Dual Culture

Malaysia-Singapore Airlines was set up in 1966 and then separated in 1972 into its two constituent airlines given the two governments' differing goals. Malaysia preferred to give priority to domestic routes but Singapore preferred the airline to focus on operating internationally. The service excellence and efficiency principles that underlie SIA's dual strategy were developed at that time as a way for SIA to effectively compete in the unforgiving world of airlines. According to Chairman JY Pillay's statement in the 1972-73 SIA Annual Report: "Singapore Airlines is able to absorb, apply and sometimes improve the high level technology of the west, at a lower cost than western airlines, and at the same time to provide the refined and gracious service for which the East is traditionally renowned". Other key decisions followed from there; cabin crew had to be properly selected, developed and rewarded, things should be done efficiently, and profits could fund further expansion and renewal of the fleet. These principles have been continually nurtured and reinforced over the years through strategic human resource management processes[4] so that they have become part of the airline's DNA.

At the airline's founding in 1972 Singapore's population was 2.2 million people, the country's gross domestic product was just US$2.7 bn, and the government budget had several other pressing priorities as the country's infrastructure was being built. The government made it clear that SIA would not be bailed out if it was making losses; it had to sink or swim. Without a home market SIA had to be "born global"[5] and to succeed by being adaptable and efficient while delivering high levels of service to demanding international travellers. Singapore's national culture emphasizes self-sufficiency and continuous learning and development, aspects that have also become embedded in SIA's organization culture. In a 1995 speech Michael Tan, Deputy Managing Director (Commercial) of SIA, recounted: "Following the restructure of Malaysia-Singapore Airlines in 1972, SIA faced a stark challenge given its relatively small home base. We had no choice but to expand and compete internationally. Right from the beginning, the Singapore government made it clear we were to operate profitably or not at all. Singapore could not afford a national carrier for the sake of pride alone"[6].

There are ongoing, multi-year internal programs such as "Transforming Customer Service" and "SOAR" (Service Above All the Rest)[7], as well as internal communications that reinforce the culture of customer orientation and frugality. SIA's ability to maintain continuous innovation and service excellence as it simultaneously implements tight cost control is facilitated by a number of factors; an organization culture that encompasses both, strategic human development processes that develop and reward individuals along these lines, and internal processes and systems that are lean, adaptable, and customer-oriented[8].

Janus Strategy at SIA

SIA's strategy would not fit neatly in one of the generic strategies of cost leadership, differentiation, and/or niche[9]. It is also not "stuck in the middle" however, a risk that the initiator of generic strategies Professor Porter warned about. This is because there is a difference between trying to achieve strategies with competing demands and failing, in the end achieving neither; or achieving both strategies, but in terms of different dimensions, which is what SIA has done. SIA's ingenious solution was that the company would be a premium-service, differentiated airline in any process or interaction that the customer experiences; but would also be a cost leader in any back-office or underlying support function that the customer does not directly experience.

One way to describe the airline's Janus strategy is that SIA simultaneously achieves both differentiation (externally) and low cost (internally), thereby finding a way to transcend the long-standing contradictions between the two generic strategies. The four paradoxes we discussed in the previous chapter are part of how this is accomplished. The Table below indicates how these paradoxes relate to key functions of the airline such as marketing strategy and strategic human resource management[10].

Achieving differentiation at low cost at Singapore Airlines
Marketing strategy centers on a positioning of service excellence, superior quality and brand equity (image of the "Singapore Girl" as the brand ambassador symbolizing Asian hospitality). Initial training is twice as long as industry average, but reduces future costs by inculcating a culture that combines customer orientation with frugality and efficiency. Market positioning supports differentiated image
Strategic human resource management aligns people development and service levels with brand promise. Process involves stringent selection and recruitment, investment in initial and ongoing training, setting up delivery teams, empowering the front line staff to control quality, and motivating through rewards and recognition. Process strengthens employee identification with airline which reduces employee turnover and fosters discretionary effort, both of which enhance quality and reduce costs
Operations strategy aligns in-flight experience with promise of service excellence (e.g. gourmet cuisine and crew behaviors such as personalization of customer interactions and going the extra mile on service). Aspects of operations such as young fleet, open innovation through things such as app development competitions, and outsourced parts of IT function reduce operating costs while supporting quality of service
Innovation strategy combines fast adoption of technology together with internal development of offerings to support service excellence. Also involves both centralized and decentralized innovation process to ensure relevance and ability to implement new offerings smoothly. SIA leads on innovations that impact the customer and follows on innovations related to support functions or that the customer does not directly experience. This and other organizational choices enable cost effective service excellence
SIA's *corporate-level strategy* is one of related diversification. It involves market listing of subsidiaries so that all parts of the business are under market discipline; subsidiaries have to be outward-oriented and performance focused rather than being allowed to create fiefdoms, corporate inertia and sunk costs
National infrastructure supports SIA's integrated strategy. Changi Airport offers both high quality as well as lower charges to airlines that use it than leading competing airports; Singaporean culture supports continuous development and self-sufficiency. The country is both a technology hub as well as a nation that appreciates gourmet cuisine. All this feeds into the success of the airline that is itself self-sufficient, and has never received any direct subsidies from the state

Table 6.1. How functional strategies enable Janus strategy

Yet another way to appreciate how SIA's Janus strategy is achieved, is through an activity systems map shown below[11].

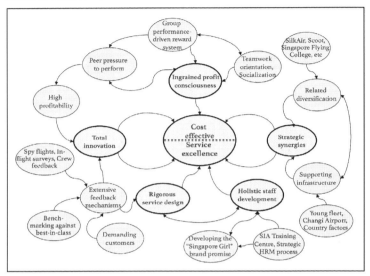

Figure 6.1. Activity systems map of SIA

In the middle is "cost effective service excellence", the core competence of SIA. This competency is strategically important and central to how SIA competes, especially because it satisfies the **VRIO** criteria: it is valuable to the customers, rare in the industry, difficult to imitate, and the airline is appropriately organized to exploit this competency[12]. Around cost effective service excellence are five "pillars", interrelated capabilities that support the core. Around these pillars, are various organizational activities that operationalize and enable the pillars[13]. Activity maps such as this one portray systemic alignment across operations and indicate how operations relate to particular capabilities and core competencies.

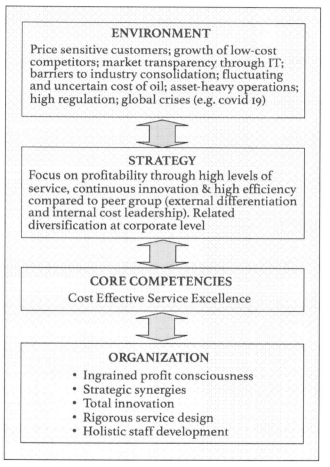

Figure 6.2. ESCO strategic alignment at Singapore Airlines

In terms of the ESCO strategic alignment model[14] shown above, the content of the activity systems map relates to the "C" (competencies, SIA's cost effective service excellence) and "O" (organization, the five pillars and the related activities). By portraying this information in an ESCO model, we can get a clearer idea of SIA's strategic alignment. This model suggests that strategy has to be appropriate for environmental conditions, that there have to be appropriate core competencies to support the strategy, and that organizational choices have to be able to deliver the competencies needed. An ESCO model for SIA could therefore be represented in Figure 6.2[15].

SIA is both aligned and also embraces paradoxical thinking, as a way to accomplish a strategy that integrates differentiation and cost leadership, two generic strategies what would normally be considered distinct and contradictory. SIA's operations involve conscious, careful choices that operationalize important aspects of both of these generic strategies, and investments that contribute to both sides of this Janus strategy. In the previous chapter we examined strategy realization through paradoxes. In this chapter we added the perspectives of functional strategy choices, activity maps and the ESCO model. Each provides a piece of the puzzle of how SIA has integrated two conventionally competing generic strategies. The six elements in Table

6.2 provide yet another useful integrative lens of examining how SIA can implement such a strategy.

Align but embrace paradox	Tight alignment across operations as shown by functional strategy choices, ESCO model and activity systems map. At the same time, operations display four paradoxes: cost effective service excellence, centralized and decentralized innovation, being a follower and a leader, and standardization as well as personalization
Be a Janus strategist	SIA's executives focused from very beginning on both service excellence as well as on efficiency; and fostered a culture and organizational processes that encompass both. Management rotation enables big-picture, corporate rather than parochial outlook; continuous training and development for everyone contributes to fresh mindset rather than inertia
Make dual strategic moves	Examples include SIA training its staff for more than twice as long as industry average, investing in its own wine cellar, and creating pressurized tasting facilities for its cuisine that simulate flight conditions. Such investments enhance differentiation, and while they may mean higher costs in the short term, they reduce costs in the long term
Use tech to both exploit and explore	SIA's technology investments such as the digital innovation blueprint, part of its transformation program initiated in 2017, aim to both raise operational optimization and efficiency, but also strengthen customer service and personalization. The airline's policy of maintaining a young fleet raises both efficiency (eg lower fuel and servicing costs) and service excellence in terms of enhanced customer flying experience
Design agile organization	SIA organization culture encompasses adaptability and continuous improvement, as inculcated by training processes, socialization, and national culture. The organization design is lean and the airline continuously seeks to finetune and optimize processes. The airline's digital innovation blueprint encompasses agile methodologies
Leverage business networks	Related diversification across SIA, SilkAir and Scoot subsidiaries affords strategic synergies; this network increases economies of scale and scope while also increasing connectivity for flyers. SIA partners with technology, research and higher education institutions to support and advance its organization change programs. The airline maintains an extensive network of business partners as part of its Krisflyer frequent flyer program, both enhancing options for its customers as well as gaining income from loyalty-related transactions

Table 6.2. The six elements of Janus strategy at Singapore Airlines

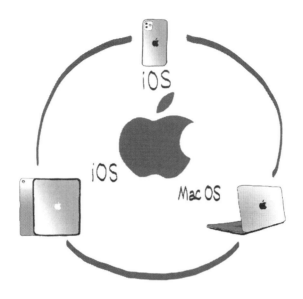

Synergies across devices via the operating system at Apple;
simultaneously reduce costs, enhance market power,
strengthen the ecosystem and improve customer experience.
An example of one of the six elements of Janus strategy,
using technology ambidextrously to both exploit current
resources and competencies (enhance efficiency and
reliability in this case) and explore (create strategic options
and enhance customer experience)

7

Janus Strategy at Apple Inc

Apple Inc has revolutionized the personal electronics, telecoms, computer and media industries through both product and business model innovations[1]. The company has accelerated the blurring of industry boundaries through its hardware that embodies convergent technologies; and its integrated ecosystem of hardware, software and services grants the company significant market power; with outstanding performance results. In mid-2020 the company was worth US$1.6 bn. Its revenues in 2019 were US$ 260bn, with net profits of US$ 55bn, a 21% profit margin. Its cash was at US$ 206bn, despite declaring cash dividends over the previous few years[2].

The late Steve Jobs was the architect of Apple's business model. With his passing in October 2011, many wondered about the fate of Apple. Yet, the company performed exceptionally well over the following decade. It managed to balance intense efficiency in operations (by some measures the highest efficiency levels in its peer group), with award-winning innovation and outstanding product design, both of which create customer loyalty and command premium pricing. This combination begs conventional wisdom which maintains that if a company's competitive advantage is based on intense efficiency or low cost, it won't invest beyond what's necessary in innovation, design, or service and will strive to cut costs everywhere along its value chain. Conversely, conventional wisdom holds that a company competing on differentiation through innovation, outstanding design, or service excellence will not be able to achieve comparatively high levels of efficiency since these capabilities are costly to develop and maintain.

Apple however has achieved both, and it is worth asking how. This strategy, if successfully executed, represents a shift of the iso-value curve to the right in any industry it is employed in, not just movement along such a curve where most competitors are positioned. An understanding of this type of Janus Strategy offers important lessons for strategists in terms of breaking the trade-offs that are conventionally assumed to constrain strategic choices and to lock firms in single generic strategies.

Two Faces of Janus: Exceptional Innovation at Low Cost

By 2020, Apple had topped the Boston Consulting Group's global innovation rankings for 15 out of the 16 most recent years[3]. The company is known for its product design capability and business model innovation in terms of the platform model, integration of hardware, software and services[4]. Yet, not many are aware that Apple integrates differentiation and low cost strategies, as shown in Table 7.1.

Differentiation strategy	Low cost strategy
Indicators of differentiation	Indicators of efficiency
Innovation rankings; innovation and design awards; highly desirable offerings	Higher inventory and receivables turnover; higher revenues and profits per employee
Ability to command premium prices and consistently achieve exceptional returns	Lower R&D intensity while company is recognised as a leading innovator
Organizational configurations	Organizational configurations
Innovation strategy; deep collaboration approach, centralized innovation process in California	Strategic focus in terms of product-markets, types of products, and product features enhances efficiency
People strategy; hiring the best people and motivating them to excel (location advantage in Silicon Valley)	Distributed org design; high value-added functions controlled in California, manufacturing outsourced to cheapest locations
Marketing strategy; brand image of maverick creativity; Investment in Apple Stores in high profile locations	Synergies from related diversification in terms of industries as well as interconnected products
Apple's proprietary ecosystem allows market power, pricing control and customer capture	Intense focus on supply chain efficiency (less warehouses, reduction of supplier numbers)
Historically, Steve Jobs' leadership; demanding, perfectionist, visionary. Tim Cook continued quality focus	Flat, lean organization, simplified processes and less bureaucracy increase efficiency

Table 7.1. Dimensions of Janus strategy at Apple Inc

Apple's differentiation is not hard to understand. The company chooses which technologies to ride based on keen market insight. It acquires young tech companies to get the emerging technologies that it needs in fields such as artificial intelligence, augmented reality, mapping and healthcare[5]. It focuses on developing innovation and design capability through having the best people and pushing them hard. It has a "deep collaboration"[6] approach via its centralized innovation processes in its campus in California. It invests in clever branding to maintain its premium positioning. It creates barriers to entry for competitors and barriers to exit for customers through building product constellations rather than stand-alone offerings. It wields market power that allows it to charge premium prices. What is harder to understand is how all this can be done at industry-leading efficiency levels.

First, increasing efficiency was a key goal of Jobs when he recruited the current CEO, Tim Cook in 1998 from Compaq to be Apple's chief operating officer. The goal was to make Apple more efficient than the traditional cost leader, Dell. Cook was instrumental in driving efficiency by streamlining Apple's manufacturing processes, supply chain and distribution operations. Soon after moving to Apple, Cook rationalized the warehouses for finished products, reasoning that "if you have closets, you'll fill them up". He also cut the number of key suppliers from 100 to 24, enhancing Apple's bargaining power; and asked them to set up shop near Apple's facilities so that components could be delivered just-in-time and manufacturing time slashed[7].

Apple's efficiency is as much due to strategic focus and simplicity however, as to supply chain rationalization. The company strives to keep a lean structure, and is focused in terms of target market, product line and product design. First, Apple aims mainly for the consumer market as opposed to the B2B sector, allowing the company to simplify its investments and operations and focus on what it does best. The market proposition in the consumer sector focuses on coolness, desire, and fun, elements alien to corporate buyers who are accountable for IT investments and go for reliability, specifications and value.

Second, the focused product line preserves management attention, facilitates marketing and increases negotiating power over suppliers. Apple chose not to produce printers and scanners for example given the narrow margins of these products. Rather than offering several models of the iPhone with an array of different functions, as for example the deposed market leader Nokia and current competitors such as Samsung do, Apple offers one main model of the iPhone which is regularly updated. After Jobs returned to Apple in 1997, at a time when the company was at risk of bankruptcy, he terminated two thirds of development projects since he judged them as not having the potential to deliver groundbreaking products. During his first management meeting after his return, dressed in shorts and sneakers and bearing stubble, Jobs exclaimed that Apple was in trouble because the products sucked and had no sex any more in them[8]. That was a call to re-focus on what had made Apple initially successful, the desirability of the products.

Thirdly, simplicity in the design and features of the products that Apple does produce. The designs are both streamlined and limited in number and include only a few features that buyers will actually use. In making these difficult choices (of what to focus on, and which features are best to include out of the hundreds of potential features), Apple becomes aligned with its customers' usage patterns, increasing value for the customer, whilst at the same time decreasing the cost of production through simplicity in design and rationalization of features.

Fourth, simplicity and efficiency are complemented by technology synergies in terms of Apple's use of its own operating system across its devices. The operating system of its iPhone and iPad is the iOS, which is a simpler version of macOS, the operating system for its laptops. In this way average costs of maintaining and updating the operating system are reduced since they can be shared across devices. User experience is enhanced through higher inter-operability and linkages across devices. A further effect of this technology strategy is that users become more deeply embedded in Apple's ecosystem, thus increasing the "stickiness" of this ecosystem, and in strategic terms mitigating users' bargaining power against the company and enhancing Apple's market power.

Fifth, Apple's own organization design is flat and bureaucracy is eschewed. As Jobs explained, Apple "is organized as a startup. One person is in charge of iPhone OS software, one person is in charge of Mac hardware, one person is in charge of iPhone hardware engineering, another person is in charge of worldwide marketing, another person is in charge of operations"[9]. Apple retains control of the functions that matter (design, innovation and partly distribution through its Apple Stores), while outsourcing most of the functions that can be provided by others more efficiently (such as manufacturing).

As with other elements of its strategy, Apple has ignored popular pronouncements such as that companies should locate several R&D facilities around the world, near their main markets, and engage in global transfer of learning. Rather than disperse its operations around the world, innovation at Apple takes place in a single space, the magic cauldron at One Infinite Loop in California. By hiring the best and co-locating them in the innovation melting pot of Apple's campus, Apple achieves extraordinary results, with only a fraction of innovation spending as percentage of revenues as compared to other large tech companies. Apple's R&D intensity ratio is at 5%, as compared to Microsoft at 14%, Intel at 21%, or Alphabet at 15%[10]. Tim Cook described Apple's philosophy as follows: "We are constantly focusing on innovating ... We believe in saying no to thousands of projects, so that we can really focus on the few that are truly important and meaningful to us. We believe in deep collaboration and cross-pollination of our groups, which allow us to innovate in a way that others cannot. And frankly, we don't settle for anything less than excellence in every group in the company, and we have the self-honesty to admit when we're wrong and the courage to change"[11].

Ratio	Apple Inc	Industry-Comp Hardware	Sector-Technology	S&P 500
Revenue per employee	$2.913m	$0.616m	$0.601m	$0.618m
Net income per employee	$0.624m	$0.107m	$0.112m	$0.053m
Inventory turnover	40.9	21.9	10.1	8.2
Receivable turnover ratio	13.8	5.5	6.6	3.8
Return on equity (5 year average)	46.6%	40.5%	19.2%	11.7%
Operating margin (5 year average)	27.3%	23%	21.5%	10.8%
Net margin (5 year average)	21.8%	17.9%	15.9%	7.1%

Table 7.2. Comparative performance metrics at Apple Inc

Other key metrics shown in Table 7.2 indicate that Apple is both more efficient and also more profitable than competitors. For example, the company turns over its inventory 40.9 times per year, twice as many as the hardware industry, four times as many as the technology sector, and five times as many as companies in the S&P 500[12]. Apple is also much more efficient in dealing with receivables. Apple's efficiency of its human resources is also shown in terms of revenues per employee of nearly US$3m, and net profits per employee of US$624,000. These figures are multiples above the industry, sector and S&P500. Apple's efficiency and market power translate to higher returns, as the comparative figures of return on equity, and operating and net margins show.

Apple's strategy and performance are supported by tight strategic alignment, as can be shown through the ESCO model in figure 7.1. Despite its tight alignment, Apple displays little inertia in terms of the evolution of its business model over time. The company went from an initial focus on hardware to building an ecosystem of hardware, software and services. In doing so it moved from primarily closed, proprietary technology standards to selective openness, to fuel its platform business model for example by allowing developers to sell their products on the Apple store and other companies to produce complementary accessories. It went from largely internal innovation to selective acquisitions to gain access to emerging technologies. All this amounts to what might be called strategic agility.

ENVIRONMENT

Intense competition in consumer electronics, software, services & computing segments; emergence of imitators in hardware and platform business model; blurring of industry boundaries, fast pace of innovation, commoditization trends in hardware

STRATEGY

Related diversification in all above segments; premium market positioning; expanding revenue streams and distribution channels (retail); selected acquisitions to gain technology; competing through largely proprietary standards and integration among offerings (ecosystem); selective openness in standards to enhance platform strategy

CORE COMPETENCIES

Design innovation; integration of hardware and software across offerings; creation of ecosystem

ORGANIZATION

Innovation and performance-oriented culture; centralized innovation; functional organization design; close collaboration among functions; flat, lean organization structure; simplified organizational processes; aiming to recruit best talent available; employee share ownership scheme

Figure 7.1. ESCO strategic alignment at Apple Inc

Dealing with Market Vagaries Through Market Power

The five forces model has been essential to strategic thinking and analysis for the last four decades[13]. The idea is that the stronger the forces in an industry, the less the profits that can be made, since the players compete away potential returns. The goal of any strategy therefore would be to enable the company to shield itself from industry forces, and in some cases, to even shape these forces, so that it can increase its profitability.

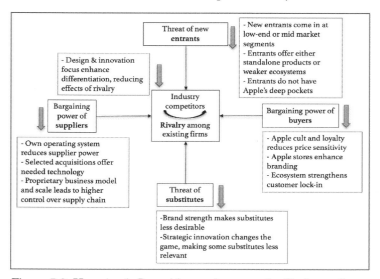

Figure 7.2. How Apple Inc mitigates the strength of industry forces

Figure 7.2 shows how Apple's way of doing business mitigates the impact of industry forces on the company, allowing outstanding financial performance.

Apple's strategy and operational choices have created certain conditions that mitigate the impact of industry forces on the company, allowing it to safely navigate the competitive rapids. Firstly, Apple can effectively mitigate rivalry by not playing the game of price competition. Because of the exceptional design of its products, and continuous innovation, it can sustain its differentiation, which enables it to keep charging a premium price and to fund further innovations (achieving a virtuous circle). Apple owns its operating system, so does not have to pay high premiums to Microsoft or other companies. It makes selected acquisitions of companies whose technology it wants (such as high-end memory chips), a more efficient way to acquire the technology than developing it in-house, assuming the acquisition is at a reasonable price. By targeting smaller companies that it can digest easily, Apple limits the financial risk of the acquisition and also the possibility that there will be a bidding war that would drive the price up. Apple does not acquire to grow or to enter an industry; but to gain access to valuable knowledge that supports its own competencies and strategy.

Further, Apple's brand power, purchasing volumes, and mode of competition in terms of value constellations within a business model built on proprietary technology (instead of stand-alone products and services using technologies owned by others), further enables it to reduce the power of suppliers. Buyers' bargaining power is reduced, since price is not the main criterion in their buying decision. Strategic innovation at Apple creates new market space and reduces the threat of substitutes. Apple's cult brand, fueled by its own Stores and its value constellation of products and services, means that buyers are willing to pay a premium price for Apple products.

Finally, the threat of new entrants is always there; but these new entrants would likely enter at the commodity side of the business rather than the premium, innovative side, They also have not developed the ecosystem that Apple has, competing instead on stand-alone products and services which puts them at a disadvantage in relation to Apple. All of these mean that Apple can make super-normal profits in industries where others are losing their shirts.

A lot of the discussion about Apple's strategy and organizational choices that enable the company to compete so effectively already alludes to key aspects of the six elements of Janus strategy. It is worth however making this more explicit, as shown in Table 7.3.

Align but embrace paradox	Apple displays both change and stability. The company shifted its business model from hardware to building an ecosystem of hardware, software and services. From closed, proprietary technology to selective openness. From conventional to platform and network business model. At the same time, it retained its core values of customer orientation, innovation and simplicity over the decades.
Be a Janus strategist	The late Steve Jobs, the architect of Apple's business model, and the current CEO, Tim Cook, wanted to create both an extremely efficient organization, as well as to innovate and enhance the customer experience. They aimed to solve complex problems in simple ways, such as to presenting complex technology in zen-style designs. The company's investments in emerging technologies and yet to be launched products display an emphasis on both exploitation and exploration
Make dual strategic moves	Apple acquires several young companies that have technology competencies it wants to invest in; such as artificial intelligence, virtual and augmented reality, mapping and healthcare. Acquisitions of a relatively small size are both an effective way to gain the technology, as well a a cheaper way than developing the technology itself
Use tech to both exploit and explore	Apple's operating system, in its different guises, underlies its constellation of offerings; in this way the considerable development cost is spread and shared across devices; and at the same time provides the user friendliness and design the users are accustomed to, improving the customer experience
Design agile organization	Apple employs a flat, functional-type organization design, despite its vast size. The company's focus in terms of markets / products / features enables economies of scale and scope and makes best use of scarce resources such as management attention and innovative capacity. Being a network organization enables both focus on critical functions as well as lower cost through the use of Apple's huge market power
Leverage business networks	Apple is a network organization, outsourcing everything except critical functions (design, branding, distribution). It controls quality and wields market power through partnering with core suppliers. Its app store is a conduit for thousands of developers to market their apps that in turn strengthen Apple's ecosystem, brand power, and increase the company's performance

Table 7.3. The six elements of Janus strategy at Apple Inc

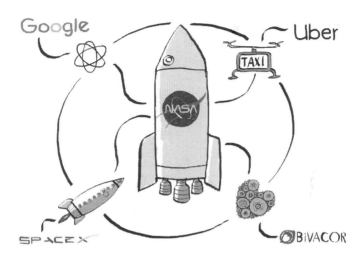

Through the commercial network model, NASA leverages limited resources to gain frontier technologies; and also disseminates such technologies to industry. An example of one of the six elements of Janus strategy, leveraging business networks, and also of using technology ambidextrously. Over time, the shift in business models from the traditional hierarchical to the inter-governmental and then to the commercial network models demonstrates strategic agility

8

Strategic Agility at NASA

NASA captures the popular imagination. It is also not the first organization that comes to mind when thinking of agility. Appearances can deceive, however. In the next two chapters we will explore how NASA has remained the pre-eminent space agency in the world, with huge ambitions for deep space travel including human journeys to Mars, and thus far the only national space agency to have put boots on the moon. NASA has accomplished its leading position through strategic agility, the ability to shift its business model over time to remain competitive; and through implementing the six elements of Janus strategy. In this chapter we examine NASA's evolution in business models from the traditional, hierarchical model to the inter-governmental partnership model and finally to the commercial network model[1]. In the next chapter we examine how Janus leadership and other elements of Janus strategy, distributed in the agency, have fostered this strategic agility. These two chapters are informed by my executive development and research work with the agency since 2013 and by the various articles co-authored with agency executives over the past few years as cited in the chapter notes.

Strategic Challenges at NASA

Spurred by the cold war, during the Apollo program in the 1960s NASA's funding rose to 4.5% of the federal budget[2], peaking at US$5,250 m in 1965[3] (the equivalent of US$34bn in 2020 dollars). Shortly after the first moon landing in 1969, when the space race was won, NASA's budget declined to US$3bn by 1975. At US$25.2 bn, the agency's 2021 budget stands at 0.5% of the federal budget[4]. As NASA faced funding restrictions while its mission aspirations grew bolder, it had to find ways to accomplish more with less.

Further, the Commercial Space Launch Act of 1984 (and amendments in 1988 and 2004) called for government agencies such as NASA to support and foster the development of commercial space. This Act marked the beginning of an ongoing push for the growth and development of commercial space by government. This shift not only necessitates a more outward-looking, collaborative way of operating by NASA as the agency has to work with commercial actors; but also calls for greater ambitions to allow commercial space organizations to populate low-earth orbit activities while

NASA leverages its resources to look beyond to deep space.

NASA has to operate in a radically changed environment. Once monopolised by state actors, the space industry is now a global, multi-faceted, multi-stakeholder endeavor, where commercial rather than state activity accounts for the lion's share of value. In 2019 the space industry was worth US$415 bn[5], only around 20% of which was due to global government spending[6]. Re-usable launch vehicles such as those developed by Space-X and Blue Origin, the availability of lower-cost nano-satellites weighing 10kg or less, and more efficient propulsion systems all fuel this marketization trend. The industry is projected by Morgan Stanley to grow to over US$ 1 trillion by 2040[7] largely driven by commercial products, services, infrastructure, and support industries. Commercial space activities and offerings will further develop within low earth orbit, up to 2,000 km from earth.

NASA has to invest its limited funds on where it can make the most difference. A fundamental challenge for the agency is therefore to successfully shift its efforts from missions closer to home and low earth orbit, that can be addressed by the commercial sector, toward deep space exploration. This involves accomplishing further manned missions to the moon where permanent facilities can be set up as a gateway for manned missions to Mars and beyond.

The emergence of commercial space goes hand in hand with an accelerating pace of technology development, as indicated for example by the number of patents granted to innovators, leaps in processing power and associated technologies such as artificial intelligence. This means that the multiple frontier technologies necessary for successful space-faring, particularly human space travel beyond low earth orbit, cannot be all developed by a single organization such as NASA. Sustaining NASA's space leadership calls for a new way of organizing and competing.

Strategic Agility at NASA

NASA has evolved over time from a traditional model during the Apollo era[8] to the transitional, partnership model fostered by the building of the International Space Station launched in 1998, and several years of planning prior to that; to today's commercial network model initiated by the Commercial Resupply Program from 2006 onwards. Each of these phases was characterized by emphasis on different organizational capabilities, cultural orientation and technology strategy. This has been an evolutionary process, with each new phase building on the previous one rather than a wholesale change of paradigm. Gradual adaptations however eventually create a markedly different business model and logic through which business is conducted.

Business model	Traditional, hierarchical model	Transitional model through inter-gov't partnerships	Commercial network model
Archetypal project	Apollo Program (1961-1975)	International Space Station (1993-present)	Commercial Resupply & Commercial Crew Programs (2006-present)
Organization capabilities	Capability focus on developing and monitoring engineering specifications, contractor supervision, and large systems integration	Capabilities incorporate learning how to collaborate effectively with international partners in inter-governmental partnerships	Focus on public-private partnerships and definition of end goals rather than detailed specs. Agency becomes catalyst for industry capability development
Cultural orientation	Culture characterized by a sense of technical superiority and exceptionalism. Agency exercises its positional authority	Cost consciousness and partnering with others take root in organization culture. Agency acts as orchestrator and influencer of a cluster of inter-governmental agencies	Commercial awareness and openness to industry-sourced solutions in addition to internally developed solutions. Open innovation programs initiated
Technology strategy	Focus on agency driven investments and unitary engineering architecture. Agency acts is prime contractor in cost-plus contracts and incurs total cost	Technologically, NASA leverages international public investments, distributed responsibility, and common interfaces, standards and protocols	Agency seeds technology development by industry via milestone payments, and leverages industry investments to achieve ever more ambitious missions

Table 8.1. The traditional, transitional and commercial network models at NASA

The traditional, hierarchical model. In its early days NASA served as both the prime contractor and the exclusive customer when dealing with its own contractors. NASA bought the technologies it needed with the relationship based on cost-plus contracts. NASA paid its contractors allowed costs, plus an agreed percentage of the total cost of the project as profit for the contractor. This model was employed for a few reasons. First, the frontier technologies that NASA needed were not already available on the market, they had to be developed from scratch by specialized contractors. Second, the cold war environment and the space race meant that NASA needed to have control of the resulting technology rather than the technology being made available on the market by contractors after development. Third, NASA's military heritage, and more broadly the procurement processes of government agencies at the time operated along those lines; cost-plus contracts that deliver on detailed specifications, with the agency owning the technology developed.

For the Apollo program in the 1960s NASA gave detailed specifications to contractors such as North American Aviation who built the command/service module of the Apollo spacecraft, Ford Aerospace who built the mission control, and Grunman Aircraft who built the Apollo lunar module, the landing part of the Apollo spacecraft. NASA defined what should be done and how, and incurred the total cost, purely funded by government. The owner of the resulting technology was NASA.

In this model, which predominated during the Apollo program and until the early 1990s when collaborative efforts with other national agencies to design and build the International Space Station started,

NASA focused on developing and monitoring detailed engineering specifications, effective contractor supervision, and large systems integration inherited from NASA's military roots. The relational approach was one of positional authority and hierarchy supported by the agency's culture that was characterized by a sense of technical superiority and exceptionalism. NASA engineers were positioned in contractor operations, with large amounts of control over what the contractors were doing, to ensure specifications set by NASA were met.

The technology strategy focused on agency-driven investments and a unitary engineering architecture. Culturally there was a sense of technological superiority and exceptionalism that developed from the government's efforts to attract the brightest scientists in order to accomplish the extraordinary challenge posed by President Kennedy in 1961: of getting a man on the moon and returning him safely to earth before the decade was out. The Saturn V rocket was one impressive result of this phase in NASA's development. It was flown between 1967 and 1973, was used for the first moon landing in 1969, and remains the largest and most powerful rocket ever to fly into space. The photos below show the Saturn V kept at the Johnson Space Center.

The transitional, inter-governmental partnership, model. In 1993 NASA was directed by the White House to collaborate with other nations on the design and construction of the International Space Station, creating an impetus for NASA to learn how to collaborate effectively with international government agencies including the European Space Agency (ESA), the Japan Aerospace Exploration Agency (JAXA), the Canadian Space Agency (CSA) and the Soviet Roscosmos. There were two driving forces for initiating this collaborative approach. First, a national policy of extending US global influence in the crucial domain of space faring through building international collaborations. Second, the space station was too expensive to be built by any single country; to maintain public support it would have to be a collaborative project.

The space station was a necessary step in the grand goal of launching human missions in deep space, such as a journey to Mars, that has been a key NASA aspiration for decades. The Mariner 6 and Mariner 7 unmanned crafts for example were the first craft successfully launched to gather data via a fly-by of Mars in 1969. A round-trip human journey to Mars would take around 21 months, depending on a variety of factors[9]. NASA needed to understand what would happen to the human body during extended missions in space, and the station would provide a way to gather this knowledge by stationing astronauts on the space station for long periods.

During this transitional phase, NASA honed how to function within a cluster of partners rather than being the dominant party in a supplier/buyer dyad as in the traditional model. This demanded shifts in capabilities, cultural values, and technology strategy. These shifts were the result of learning and adapting over time how to operate effectively within collaborative relationships.

Culturally, the sense of technological superiority developed over the Apollo program when NASA overcame enormous technical challenges to successfully land humans on the moon and win the space race, was still present. However, greater cost consciousness developed as the American public and politicians began questioning the amount of resources needed by the agency. Contrary to the Apollo era when funds were not an object in the effort to win the space race, now NASA had to accomplish its missions as efficiently as possible and be more explicit about its added value to society.

The sense of hierarchical pecking order of the traditional model was supplemented by a cluster of international governmental organizations, with NASA as the orchestrator and influencer. To borrow a phrase from the governance field, NASA now became primus inter pares, the first among equals as it negotiated with, coordinated and led the network of international space agencies to accomplish one of the most complex undertakings of humanity, designing and building the space station.

NASA's technology strategy evolved. From leveraging its own investments within a dyad and taking on all technical responsibility, NASA begun leveraging the investments of its state partners, their international public investments, within a network of agencies and with distributed technical responsibility. NASA worked with its partners on developing shared technical interfaces, standards and protocols, learning in the process how to operate within a network of state actors in inter-governmental partnerships.

The commercial network model. The network model began with the Commercial Resupply Services program that was initiated to carry cargo to the International Space Station after the space shuttle was retired. The first space shuttle flight took place in 1981. After 135 missions and 30 years of operation, the space shuttle program was terminated and the three shuttles in operation at the time were retired in 2011. A key reason for termination was due to the program's costs that were orders of magnitude higher than planned[10]. Second, the shuttle could only fly within low earth orbit, but NASA had aspirations for deep space and needed funds to develop Orion and the Space Launch System for manned missions to Mars. Given that its budget would not increase significantly, but its mission ambitions were growing, NASA had to prioritize and reallocate funds from other programs.

In 2008 NASA awarded contracts to Space X and Orbital Sciences to transport cargo to the station. Space X carried out its first resupply mission in 2012 and Orbital Sciences in 2013. On 30 May 2020, two astronauts were transported to the space station on a Falcon 9 SpaceX rocket[11]. What made this phase different was that by 2008, space-faring capabilities were being developed by industry in the open market. They were no longer the province of state actors, whose spending at the time was one third of the global space market of US$257bn[12], a proportion that continued to decrease as the total size of the industry grew. NASA wanted to use part of its budget not only to buy services it needed, such as to resupply the station with cargo, but also to use the contract-award process to spur the growth of commercial space. NASA looked for outside partners because it recognised that the expertise was now available in the open market to deliver frontier capabilities, at lower cost compared to what NASA could develop them for.

This model involved fixed-price contracts within public-private partnerships, where NASA would not exclusively own the resulting technology. Commercial partners could sell their services based on such technology to other customers. Costs are shared, with NASA paying for milestones reached. Rather than providing detailed specifications for the what and the how, NASA specifies high level goals (the what), leaving the how to the commercial partners. The goals of the Commercial Resupply Services program were to be able to deliver to the ISS and then dispose as needed of external, unpressurised cargo (parts and equipment for use on the orbiting laboratory); to deliver and then dispose of internal, pressurized cargo (food, clothing and equipment for use inside the habitable parts of the ISS); and to be able to deliver back to earth delicate pressurized cargo such as materials from experiments that took place on the ISS.

The commercial resupply program has taught NASA how to work effectively with the commercial sector and to manage ongoing public-private partnerships. Culturally this has led to a more outward-looking agency that recognises and capitalizes on the innovative capacity of the market and is open to solutions created anywhere in the network. Dealing with commercial actors has also taught NASA greater commercial awareness. This involves a focus on accomplishing things as efficiently as possible and being conscious about the costs of any given activity; a far cry from the sense of having unlimited resources during the Apollo program.

Whereas in the traditional model NASA was the primary actor in dyads between itself and its contractors, and in the transitional phase it was the primary actor in a limited network of state actors (public-public partnerships) governed by strict international agreements, in the commercial network model NASA is part of an innovative network of clusters involving a multitude of actors and public-private partnerships. This new location within a network involves a shift in perspective; rather than being the only buyer who specifies exactly what technologies are needed, with detailed specifications, NASA now makes statements of the high-level capabilities needed, and leaves it to the commercial partners to develop whatever technologies they believe can fulfil these capabilities. The innovators can then exploit these technologies commercially as they see fit, further fuelling the development of space technology and enhancing the value of the network.

NASA's technology strategy has also evolved. In the traditional model it was leveraging its own agency investments; in the transitional model it complemented its own investments with those of its international state partners (leveraged international public investments). In the network model, NASA additionally leverages the investments of any commercial entity that can develop technology that can offer the particular capabilities NASA needs, such as the investments of Space X and Blue Origin in developing re-usable rockets that significantly reduce the cost of space launches. NASA's current research partnerships include working with Uber on "urban air mobility" to identify and develop the data and tools needed to enable large scale air taxis in large cities[13]. NASA is also working with Google to advance quantum computing, so that calculations that would take the most advanced conventional computers thousands of years, can be carried out in seconds[14].

Part of this shift in NASA's way of operating is the use of open innovation. The agency now poses innovation challenges online in open competitions, crowdsourcing ingenious solutions and ideas as a complement to internal innovation efforts. Successful open innovation challenges have included competitions on the design of pressurized yet flexible astronaut gloves, ways to accurately measure the strain on materials used in space such as Kevlar straps, and better forecasting of potentially destructive solar flares. At the same time, the agency is continuing to research intractable problems such as space travel at warp speed[15].

NASA therefore takes advantage of simultaneous internal/external innovation and is now able to use innovations wherever they emerge within its networks so that it can accomplish great things such as deep space exploration, the search for extra-terrestrial life, and human journeys to Mars. NASA is currently the only organization in the world that can realistically lead in the pursuit of these goals, making this organizational reinvention fundamental for future survival of the human species. Given the space policy directive from the US Government in December 2017 directing NASA to return to manned missions to the moon as a stepping-stone for manned missions to Mars and further afield, it is vital to maintain the agency's competitiveness and leading-edge capabilities. The US government wants NASA to accomplish this through working with commercial space as much as possible[16].

A key aspect of Janus strategy is building an agile organization. While NASA has to have robust and reliable processes so that it can carry out incredibly complex and dangerous missions safely, it also has adapted its business model and way of operating substantially over time, a strategic dimension to agility[17]. In the next chapter we explore how a group of agency engineers, the NASA Pirates, challenged the agency to develop new capabilities and pushed it towards the commercial network model in the 1980s. Through the story of the pirates we will see how other elements of Janus strategy are found in NASA.

The NASA pirates were pioneers of agility. They were
engaging in agile practices since the 1980s, well before the
agile manifesto was published in 2001. Organizations of any
type and size can combine scale with flexibility if they can
create a culture that values diverse perspectives and allows
for emergence of new ways and initiatives

9

Agents of Janus: The NASA Pirates

In the previous chapter we discussed NASA's strategic agility, its ability to shift its business model including its capabilities, culture and technology strategy more than once over time. This agility owes a lot to individuals who can see far ahead, are driven by the mission, and who have the courage, persistence and energy to challenge the status quo and forge a new path ahead[1]. These are the true Janus strategists as they can think and operate simultaneously in both the present and the future; both exploiting current competencies and resources and building new ones. Such leaders are not only found at the top of organizations but at any level. They are often perceived as renegades or rebels and seen as troublemakers; difficult individuals who have to get with the program. Research at NASA's Johnson Space Center (JSC) however, suggests that we need such renegades more than we think. Far from disruptive, they can be powerful means for revitalizing and shifting organizations toward new futures.

My research associates and I learned about a group called the "NASA Pirates" as part of an ongoing research project at JSC that started in 2013. The purpose of the project is to understand how organizations can become ambidextrous, able to attend to competing demands. Over the years we conducted ethnography though long visits to the Center, management workshops, and interviews with managers, scientists and engineers. In our interviews we uncovered the story of the Pirates as a historically innovative and agile force within NASA whose effects still reverberate. This group created a new, award-winning mission control system for the Shuttle in record time, on a shoestring budget and in the face of political resistance. They were pioneers in agile practices fifteen years before agility entered the organizational vocabulary; the "agile manifesto" had not been created till 2001. We went on to seek out and interview several of the original Pirates including the Pirate leader, John Muratore; and supplemented our data through NASA's oral history interviews and other historical documents.

The Pirates story has important lessons for organizations, particularly those that want to address competing demands and aim for Janus strategy. Renegade groups can act as important revitalizing forces, offering new solutions that can future-proof organizations by transcending the limits of current systems. Organizations in turn should create fertile ground for such groups to emerge. When they form, these groups need to be protected from organizational bureaucracy, inertia and politics by high-level sponsors who can understand and appreciate what the renegades aim to achieve.

How the NASA Pirates Brought Real-Time Data Systems to Mission Control

When the young engineer John Muratore joined the Johnson Space Center in 1983 after four years in the Air Force Space Shuttle Program, he was surprised to see that the computer architecture in operation in the Shuttle mission control center was still the Apollo-era mainframe system set up in the early 1960s. Displays were monochrome, lacked graphics, and the system could handle only a limited number of simultaneous calculations, otherwise it could be overwhelmed. Any changes in functionality such as new types of calculations could take months to implement. This system mostly displayed data and left the task of data analysis and interpretation to be done manually by the flight controllers. If more computational power was needed by the flight controllers, additional personal computers were used offline[2]. The photos below show the Apollo-era mission control:

Muratore wondered whether the incumbent
mainframe system could stand up to the burgeoning

mission demands and complexity of the Shuttle program, not to mention the mission control needs of the planned International Space Station. In 1986, in the wake of the Challenger accident, Muratore's concern morphed into a strong desire to do something to elevate the capabilities of mission control so it could respond to mission demands growing in scope and complexity. Progressive budget cuts after the Apollo landings meant that the agency had to cope with ever decreasing resources.

Muratore connected with a small group of newly recruited engineers who felt the same way about the incumbent system. This small group of renegades wanted to future-proof mission control by using an open, distributed, upgradable and scalable systems architecture that could potentially incorporate not-invented-yet future technologies. Rather than mainframe computing, they wanted to use a network of personal computers that were widely available and much cheaper. The new technology model was described as "a distributed system of Unix engineering-class workstations to run a mix of online real-time expert systems, and traditional automation to allow flight controllers to perform more tasks and to capture the corporate knowledge of senior personnel"[3]. The group's concerns fell on deaf ears. The feeling in mission control was that the incumbent system had taken humans to the moon; it was highly tailored, tried and tested. Flight controllers and software engineers knew its every quirk and felt they could respond well in any emergency.

Muratore and his cohorts were undeterred. They decided to apply for a small internal grant for "new technology", and with those meagre funds they started putting together borrowed hardware and writing new code. They could only keep the hardware for 90 to 120-day cycles given government rules about using free resources from NASA suppliers[4]. They worked during lunchtimes, evenings and weekends and after about a year they took their system, composed of clusters of off-the-shelf hardware and their tailor-made code, into mission control.

After being rebuffed by the flight controllers, the legendary flight director Eugene Kranz[5], who understood what the renegades were trying to accomplish, asked the flight controllers to give the kids a chance. The renegades' system was allowed in the mission control room and continued to run seamlessly on two separate occasions when the mainframe crashed. It displayed color graphics, integrated reports on the status of Shuttle systems, and user-friendly interfaces, resulting in "dramatic new and unexpected capabilities"[6]. Flight controllers realized that they could make faster and more accurate decisions with the new system, compared to having to interpret the shapeless rows of monochrome numbers on their own screens. Over time, all the various technical systems that were required to fly the Shuttle were successfully transitioned to the renegades' system[7]. The mission control that the pirates created is pictured below:

The Pirate Paradigm: Agility Before it Was in Vogue

Over time the renegade group needed an identity. The "Pirate paradigm" whose main values are shown below, was created:

■ *When in command...COMMAND!*
■ *Be on the intellectual cutting edge of the technology of your field.*
■ *Be responsible and accountable for the results of your area.*
■ *Do not wait to be told to do something, figure it out for yourself.*
■ *Challenge everything, and steel yourself for the inevitable cynicism, opposition, rumors, false reporting, innuendo and slander.*
■ *Give lots and lots of credit and praise to your team.*
■ *Always plan for success; however, know that successful plans will tolerate occasional failure.*
■ *Push the limits of the system. Create an atmosphere of urgency for required timelines and schedules.*
■ *Break the rules, not the law. Take risks as a rule not as the exception.*
■ *Cut out unnecessary timelines, schedules, processes, reviews and bureaucracy.*
■ *Just get started, fix problems as you go along.*
■ *Always deliver more than others think is possible.*
■ *Build a product, not an organization. Outsource as much as possible.*

PIRATE PARADIGM

Figure 9.1. The pirate paradigm at NASA

Several of these values challenged the established culture of the agency that had been developed historically in the military installations that were brought together to form NASA as a civilian agency in 1958[8]. While the top three values in the paradigm were part of the dominant culture, the remaining values on the list were brought in by the pirates. The pirate movement was all about achieving results, resilience in the face of challenge, and maintaining personal responsibility. By shaping action that went beyond the established conservative culture, these values enabled innovation that brought essential, new mission control capabilities to NASA.

The Pirates' motto of "build a little, test a little, fix a little," included practices such as regular short-cycle milestones to encourage continuous improvement and experimentation; results orientation; cutting out bureaucracy and paperwork as much as possible; encouraging personal accountability and responsibility; and challenging of convention while operating in a large, rule-bound hierarchical organization. These practices were the essence of agility decades before the term became fashionable. It took great courage, persistence and commitment for the Pirates to challenge the organization culture, but it was what the organization needed to be ultimately able to operate the Shuttle program effectively and to build the International Space Station.

This way of operating would be innovative for many organizations even today and was nothing short of a revolution in the procedural, rule-bound, hierarchical culture of the agency. It was seen as an intrusion that angered many, who wanted to see the Pirates fail. The Pirates faced fierce opposition from the established order, including middle management and software developers who felt that the flight operator-Pirates, by writing their own code, were encroaching on their turf[9]. The Pirates needed their own community; a place to belong, and a buffer to the immune response of the organization. Below is a photo of the lead Pirates, and selected logos that were adopted by pirate teams working on different dimensions of the mission control project[10]:

But the Pirates did not just challenge tradition, they also heeded accumulated learning and experience. Some "greybeards", established and experienced NASA scientists and managers who understood and appreciated what the Pirates aimed to accomplish hang around the group and offered help and advice. The Pirates slowly won the quiet support of high-level sponsors, individuals such as flight director Eugene Kranz and Johnson Space Center administrator George Abbey who would step in when needed to provide top cover and clear the way for the Pirates.

In 1992, after the successful transition of the Shuttle control system, the Pirates were tasked with developing the capabilities of mission control for the planned International Space Station, whose assembly begun in 1998. The Pirates' mission control system operated at lower cost for both the Shuttle and the International Space Station programs, compared to what it initially cost to run just the Shuttle program using the Apollo-era mainframe system. In 1994 the Pirates were awarded the Vice President's Hammer Award for groups that made outstanding innovations to the functioning of government. The award recognised the Pirates' development of the new Shuttle mission control with cost savings of US$74 million in development, as well as recurring annual savings of US$22 million[11].

In 1995, during a government hearing on NASA procurement processes[12], Muratore responded to delegates' questions as follows: "as we started on the path to the Control Center I wasn't sure if I was going to be sitting here talking to you about how well this worked out or sitting here explaining to you why we did all these crazy things and took some chances with the way we were building the new Control Center. I mean, there was a lot of reluctance on people's parts to just start a new way of doing business given that the past way had been successful and we were dealing with such a critical resource and facility. ... I think the senior management at Johnson Space Center deserves a lot of credit because they let that kind of dialectic go on for a while. There was a lot of very heated disagreement... That's when we started with what we call 'the pirate revolution'. The idea of challenging the way we've done business; how we scrubbed out all of the paperwork; how we got to an approach where actually NASA was, I think, in better control of what's going on ... there is a big cultural change that has to take place and that people have to have the courage to go ahead and try that".

Renegades as Revitalizing Forces

The NASA Pirates story has important lessons for achieving Janus strategy. In particular, such groups foster diversity of thinking, revitalise organizations facing novel challenges, and help to accomplish both exploitation of current resources and competencies while building new, crucial ones, even though most people may not yet recognise the need to do so.

Novel challenges necessitate new solutions and systems, often developed by renegades. All systems have performance limits that may make them unable to deal with novel challenges. In the 1980s mainframe computing could not deliver the functionality and flexibility that distributed computing could. We are now just beginning to see the reshaping potential of artificial intelligence in industries such as financial services, healthcare, automotive, retail and education. To capitalize on AI's potential benefits, new information technologies and organizational processes are needed, rather than simply refining current systems. New approaches however are often resisted and suppressed by the established order and dominant interests, and discouraged by organizational inertia and the urgency of everyday fire-fighting.

This is when "positive deviants"[13] such as the NASA Pirates come in. These are individuals and groups who are embedded in operations, understand looming challenges, and have the expertise, motivation and vision to seek and create a better way to deal with these challenges. They are the "troublemakers" who can end up bringing essential competencies to the organization. Several organizations can attest to the value of renegade groups through their history. IBM's move to the internet[14], Lockheed Martin's fabled Skunkworks[15], and Apple's Macintosh project[16] were all led by such groups.

Organizations should create fertile ground for the emergence of renegades. To face intractable challenges and wicked problems top-down leadership is not sufficient because the solutions are not known and diverse thinking is essential. The collective intelligence of the organization and often beyond have to be tapped[17]. Many organizations focus on strategic and organizational alignment, expecting everyone to tow the line and pouncing on any signs of deviation from the norm. Tight alignment and homogeneity can foster efficiency and optimization, but also bring inherent risks. Namely, they do not allow for system evolution or revolution. An important antidote to inertia is renegade groups, or positive deviants, who via constructive dissent and innovative outputs may hold the key to step improvements.

Organizations can move toward this direction by developing an organization culture that is truly open to challenge and positive dissent; and provide seed funding and time for experimentation to positive deviants. Once they emerge, sheltering renegade groups from company bureaucracy and politics is essential; such groups should be protected from the organizational immune system. Further, organizations need to ensure that high level sponsors can connect with and support renegade groups. Without such support, the organizational immune system will pose obstacles to renegades' work and may even halt it. Finally, organizations can invest in developing leaders with an ambidextrous mindset, aiming to balance the needs of both the present as well as the future, optimization as well as creation. All these measures can help to bring about an environment that accepts positive deviance rather than suppresses it; and offers the best chance of renegade groups emerging and making a difference.

The changes that can be occasioned by renegade groups are not just incremental; the history of such groups shows otherwise. Transformational changes can be achieved because renegades challenge the status quo with credible solutions and with the intrinsic motivation to make a difference. Such motivation is also an important way of knowing that a renegade group are constructive, positive deviants rather than just anarchists who enjoy chaos or challenge for the sake of it. Because of the potential for radical change however, renegade groups often fall afoul of the establishment, even encountering outright hostility from the dominant order. One way to protect such groups is to connect them with high level sponsors who understand the value of the quest for new ways. These sponsors can offer advice, a strategic perspective, and can step in to remove obstacles from the renegades' path as needed.

The NASA Pirates officially disbanded in 2002, but their effects in the agency reverberate. They took their ways of operating with them across the organization, with several former Pirates now in leading positions across the agency and the space industry. Corporate history shows that this is not a unique, parochial case. Rather, the ability to foster such groups in any organization may make the difference between inertia and decline, or innovation and competitive advantage.

The Table below summarizes key ideas from this and the previous chapter on NASA in terms of the six elements of Janus strategy:

Align but embrace paradox	Agency operations have to be aligned, stable, reliable and efficient so that missions of increasing ambition and complexity can be accomplished as efficiently and safely as possible. At the same time, the agency has had to shift its business model over time, to sustain its internal and external alignment. This simultaneous stability and change is a paradoxical but necessary orientation
Be a Janus strategist	The lead NASA Pirates, and current leaders with a similar orientation, are archetypal Janus strategists. They see far ahead and do what is needed to advance the organization's competencies to deal with forthcoming challenges. At the same time they don't drop the ball with ongoing operations. The simultaneous present/future orientation, and exploitation/exploration efforts is what defines Janus strategists
Make dual strategic moves	The agency's open innovation program allows externally sourced solutions to be employed to address mission challenges. Such solutions are obtained by the agency faster and cheaper from the crowd rather than if they were developed internally. At the same time, the agency is working on intractable paradoxical theoretical challenges such space travel at warp speed. The simultaneous internal/external innovation is characteristic of a Janus approach
Use tech to both exploit and explore	NASA's commercial network model allows the agency to accomplish more with less by leveraging commercially available technologies and open systems architectures. In terms of projects, the mission control developed by the NASA Pirates delivered new crucial capabilities based on real time data systems and distributed architecture; as well as multi-million dollar savings both in terms of development and in recurrent, ongoing operations
Design agile organization	The agency has displayed strategic agility over the years, shifting its business model from the traditional hierarchical model to the transitional partnership model, and finally to the commercial network model. This has necessitated the evolution of the agency's capabilities, culture and technology strategy. In operational terms, the NASA Pirates brought agile practices to the agency long before the agile manifesto was published
Leverage business networks	NASA's commercial network model involves the agency working closely with industry to leverage commercial investments. The agency defines end goals and capabilities needed rather than detailed specs; and seeds development of commercial space sector. It can draw frontier knowledge and technology from wherever it is available to accomplish ambitious missions. Organizations in NASA's network such as SpaceX and Blue Origin are indispensable to the agency's current and future missions

Table 9.1. The six elements of Janus strategy at NASA

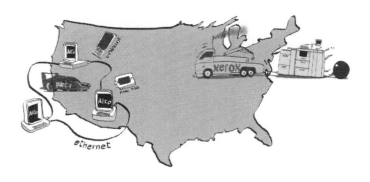

Xerox focused so much on its core business of copiers that it
failed to explore the potential of the groundbreaking
technologies of its innovation subsidiary, PARC. This is an
apt example of the Icarus paradox, brought about by the
creation of competency traps. Some of PARC's technologies
were taken up by competitors, or PARC scientists left to
create startups where Xerox did not retain a stake. Where
Xerox did keep a stake, this reduced the strategic flexibility
of startups leading to lower performance

10

Playing with Janus: Xerox and PARC

X erox was founded in 1906 as "The Haloid Photographic Company" in Rochester, NY, making photographic paper and equipment. In 1959 the company introduced the Xerox 914, the first automatic commercial copier, based on a process developed by an independent physicist in 1938 and then refined for several years. The 914 was based on a new xerography process that replaced previous methods of carbon and wet process duplication[1]. The company was renamed Haloid Xerox in 1958 and then The Xerox Corporation in 1961. The company grew fast and dominated the copier market. By the end of that year Xerox achieved $60 million in revenue, up from $32 million in 1959. "Xeroxing" became part of popular parlance. By 1968 revenues grew to $1.1 billion, and the company's employee base from 900 to 24,000. By 1970 the company held a 95% market share in the global copier market with gross margins averaging seventy to eighty percent[2].

At that point, at the dawn of the information technology era, Xerox CEO Peter McColough made a far-sighted decision to create the Palo Alto Research Center (PARC) near Stanford University. He had been appointed CEO in 1968 after leading sales and marketing for the Xerox 914. Xerox had acquired Scientific Data Systems (SDS) in 1969 as a way to enter the computer business. The company became Xerox Data Systems, and was subsequently shut down in 1975 after disappointing performance. McColough wanted to make Xerox the "architect of information" for the business office[3]. At its founding in 1970, PARC was tasked with inventing technologies for the office of the future so as to prepare Xerox for the "paperless" office that the company believed could be brought about by information technology[4]. Looking to Bell Labs as a model of the research environment that could be created, PARC sought the best scientists and created the necessary conditions to allow them to innovate. Initially PARC consisted of three laboratories focusing on Computer Science, General Science Laboratory and Systems Science, with the Optical Science Lab added a few years later. In steady state PARC consisted of around 300 individuals and had a flat organization design, with just 3 levels of hierarchy.

The first director of PARC, George Pake, a former physics professor, followed the principles of "1. Recruit the best, most creative researchers you can find. 2. Give the researchers the most supportive environment you can provide, including ample amounts of the most advanced instrumentation. Holding tight on capital spending is a foolish economy-in fact, it is a false economy ... 3. Work the business needs of the corporation into the program through selective budgetary preferences. ... make a conscious effort to imitate the best research in universities by providing an intellectual environment[5]". PARC became the mecca for top computer scientists, "like Disneyland for seven-year-olds."[6] In order to align its activities with its mission to innovate and with Xerox's strategy, PARC undertook several studies in 1971 to "review and project the state of technologies relevant for Xerox, along with an assessment of how those technologies were likely to evolve[7]". Scientists at PARC went on to develop a number of revolutionary technologies over the next fifteen years including the laser printer, object-oriented programming, the Alto personal workstation, the Bravo word processing program, graphical user interface with point and click interaction, the Ethernet, memory storage devices, email, and the local area network using optical fiber cable.

However, other than the laser printer that became a huge commercial success, Xerox did not introduce to market any of the other groundbreaking inventions. Several of the scientists who developed these technologies felt frustrated at the company's seeming reluctance to develop further these inventions into marketable products, or even to explore what the technologies could accomplish, and left to create their own companies. During the twenty-year period 1979 to 1998, there were 35 technology company spin-offs from Xerox, 30 of which were initiated by Xerox and 5 from scientists who left to start their own businesses. Of those 5, Adobe became the most successful. For the first 10 of those spin-offs during 1983 to 1991, that included Adobe, Xerox did not retain any equity. The process was described as a "laissez faire" model[8]. Xerox's spin-off model gradually became more structured, culminating in the conscious prioritization of inventions that were seen as fitting in with Xerox's business, in which the company retained a controlling stake when the companies where spun off.

Xerox's majority stake in these young, fledgling companies however turned out to be an albatross around their necks. Xerox appointed its own managers as CEOs and directors and made the companies subject to Xerox's annual budgetary cycle, with the goal of retaining control and seeking complementarities between how they developed, and Xerox's businesses[9]. This direction however was not always the most promising for the companies themselves. The spin-offs that were successful, such as Adobe, had to shift drastically their initial strategic direction and business models to align with market demand and emergent opportunities. They were able to do so because they were not subject to Xerox's control. In fact, Xerox spin-offs that had a higher number of venture capitalists on their boards performed better in terms of revenue growth and market value, whereas those with a Xerox insider as CEO performed worse[10]. The Xerox corporate paradigm and business model were used to guide the opportunities and solutions that these young companies could offer. This lens turned out to be too restrictive however[11], leading to reduced competitiveness and inertia in these companies. Xerox's failure to commercialize promising PARC technologies and gain value from them stands as one of the greatest blunders in corporate history[12]. In mid-2020, Xerox's market value hovered at $3.5 billion. Adobe's market value, based on early technology developed at PARC, was $216 billion.

In this chapter we get some insight on why it is so difficult to simultaneously compete both for today and for the future[13]; to exploit current competencies and resources, and at the same time explore for new ones; to focus on your core business, and at the same time be able to envision and imagine new businesses. To see a technology not just for what it is, and its current fit with the core business, but rather to imagine what markets the technology could create; to be able to seriously entertain the possibility that it could spawn whole new industries that may not be so related to your core business, and to want a (major) piece of that action. In short, we will see why Janus strategy is so tricky to achieve.

Dominant Logic and Core Business at Xerox

There were three key obstacles to Xerox taking advantage of the potentially industry-shaping inventions coming out from PARC: first, the company's dominant logic[14], the paradigm through which management saw the business and market options; second, the disjointed nature of PARC and its inventions from the rest of the business; and third, the organizational tensions between PARC and headquarters.

Xerox's paradigm focused on the copier business. By 1980 Xerox had revenues of $8.2 billion; but only $300 million came from its office products division, with the lion's share coming from copiers. Revenue was expected to increase to US$17 billion by 1985, with the office products division accounting for just $1 billion of this amount[15]. Xerox's value proposition was "high quality copies in high volume at a low monthly lease rate"[16]. The business model depended on developing machines that could make as many copies as possible fast and reliably. As Xerox's CEO at the time observed: "our profits came from how many copies were made on those machines. If a copier was slow in generating copies, that was money plucked out of our pocket"[17].

Xerox targeted the high end of the market; a Xerox 914 copier in 1966 for example cost $27,500. This would be equivalent to $222,000 in 2020. However, copiers "could be rented for twenty-five dollars monthly, plus at least forty-nine dollars' worth of copies at four cents each"; maintained by over a thousand repairmen who were "ready to answer a call on short notice to avoid losing money"[18]. This business model reinforced the paradigm that "Xerox sees its business forte primarily as providing services and systems to the business office, and not as a component or subsystem supplier"[19]. Given the company's virtual monopoly in the copier business at the time, and its fat profit margins and growth prospects, Xerox executives focused on growing and protecting it. The more copies lucrative corporate customers were making, the higher the revenues and profits of Xerox[20].

Apart from the invention of the laser printer, the novel technologies created at PARC were seen by Xerox management to have little explicit or direct relevance to the copier business. PARC had been intentionally set up as a separate operation to shield it from the corporate paradigm and to enable ground-breaking inventions, a move referred to as "structural ambidexterity"[21]. According to John Seely Brown, former Chief Scientist at Xerox and Director of PARC for almost two decades, "At PARC, we were given the freedom to invent what we wanted and build whatever we needed in order to make possible whatever we dreamed. We had a simple mantra: 'Build what you need; use what you build.' This gave us a tremendous grounding for many of the things that we invented"[22].

PARC engineer Bob Metcalfe who then founded 3Com recounted, "there wasn't any hierarchy. We built out our own tools. When we needed to publish papers, we built a printer. When we needed to edit the papers, we built a computer. When we needed to connect computers, we figured out how to connect them. We had big budgets. Unlike many of our brethren, we didn't have to teach. We could just research. It was heaven ... We built a computer and it was a beautiful thing ... We developed our computer language, our own display, our own language. It was a gold-plated product. But it cost $16,000, and it needed to cost $3,000".[23] $16,000 in 1973 when the Alto was created at PARC would be $96,000 in 2020, something far beyond the reach of the retail market and of most small or medium sized enterprises.

Missed Opportunities

PARC's inventions were inherently uncertain in terms of market potential, especially in the fast-moving segments of the technology industry. Xerox was only interested in advancing and commercializing technologies that in its view could in time be worth billions, and that were connected to its core business, copiers. Xerox for example decided against commercializing Notetaker, a computer-based word processor developed in 1976 by Larry Tesler, PARC principal scientist. This was partly because Xerox had set up a computer engineering facility in Dallas, headed by Robert Potter, which was seen as competing rather than collaborating with PARC[24]. "In addition to animosity, Dallas ignored PARC because Potter could not imagine a big market for advanced computer-based word processors"[25]. After inventing Notetaker, Tesler spent a lot of time flying around the country trying to convince Xerox executives to support and commercialize his product. He recalled, "Xerox executives made all kinds of promises, 'We'll buy 20,000 just talk to this executive in Virginia, then talk to this executive in Connecticut,' after a year I was ready to give up"[26]. In December 1979 Tesler was asked to show Steve Jobs some of the technologies that PARC was developing, including the Alto computer that featured network connectivity, bitmap display, a mouse, WYSIWYG (what you see is what you get) word processor, windows and a graphical user interface. Shortly after, Tesler was lured to Apple.

Other examples include AstraNET and Bravo. AstraNET, invented by Andrew Ludwick at PARC, connected several workstations together with a single host cable. Xerox rejected his proposal to commercialize it because it was seen as insignificant in terms of revenues. "Since I thought that the market size of AstraNet was at most $100 million, no one at Xerox wanted to invest any time in the technology"[27]. Charles

Simonyi helped to create Bravo, the first WYSIWYG text editor. Bravo had been used in PARC since 1974 and was so popular that relatives of PARC employees would come in at night to use it[28]. However, Bravo was never commercialized. Simonyi hoped that a senior manager would recognize its market potential, but later realized that "it was naive to assume such an executive would come from Xerox"[29].

When technologies beyond copiers and imaging were commercialized, they often did not do very well. Star, a workstation for the corporate market that could connect with other computers by Ethernet to form a system of interlinked computers connected to a printer, was launched in 1981. Star was a closed system comprised of Xerox proprietary technology. This was the first commercially available set of workstations to feature a graphical user interface, icons and a mouse and offered unprecedented ease of use. However, the Star system was expensive, "initially offered at $16,995; the network requisite facilities and shared printer raised the cost for a three-user system to over $100,000" and was mainly sold to Fortune 1000 companies via a direct sales force[30]. $16,995 in 1981 would be over $50,000 in 2020, when a three-user system would cost nearly $300,000.

Cheaper competing products were about to enter the market. PARC researchers were aware of this development[31], but Xerox managers did not appear to appreciate the implications. Xerox retained both the uncompetitive price for the Star and targeted executive clients who were likely not the direct users; at the time their assistants would prepare documents for them. Four months after the Star was introduced, IBM released the 5150, a personal computer available for just $1,565 and aimed at the broader market, "designed for business, school and home"[32]. Although the 5150 was not as technically advanced and did not have features such as icons, a graphical user interface or a mouse, its market entry contributed to the demise of the Star[33]. Steve Jobs, who incorporated many of the Alto's features in the first Apple computer, thought that "Xerox could have owned the entire computer industry, could have been the IBM of the nineties, could have been the Microsoft of the nineties"[34]. Alluding to PARC's contribution to information technology research and Xerox's failure to benefit from most of these inventions, former PARC director George Pake noted that "my friends tease me by calling PARC a national resource"[35].

Culture Clash and Rampant Politics Cause Tensions

PARC's organization design was intentionally informal, organic, and flat, resembling a university department and granting considerable autonomy to scientists. Xerox on the other hand had a more formal, hierarchical, mechanistic structure with defined processes and rules. The two were diametrically opposed in many ways. PARC scientist Adele Goldberg recalled that on corporate training, other employees treated her differently; "as soon as they found out I was from PARC, they weren't as nice anymore"[36]. The Economist put it as follows: "the people at PARC were treated like inmates of a zoo - admired and fed but rarely let loose"[37]. PARC chief scientist John Seely Brown recalls that there were annual meetings intended to bring PARC and Xerox together; "...such formal exchanges took place in annual 'gap closure' meetings, when the two sides got together and contemplated the distance between them before returning to their separate spheres. Because these meetings were always struggles over power and turf conducted with varying amounts of passive-aggressive behavior, the gaps were almost impossible to close"[38].

After 18 months in the Nixon administration as Assistant Secretary of Commerce for Science and Technology, and before moving to MIT to direct the Center for Advanced Engineering Study, Myron Tribus became Senior Vice President for Research and Engineering at Xerox from 1970 to 1974. He recalled: "I was used to the politics at Washington, but at Xerox it was way worse. In Washington, you knew your adversaries and accepted they would work against you. At Xerox, you only found out who was not on your side after you noticed the knife in your back"[39].

PARC scientist John Ellenby was responsible for the Futures Day presentation in 1977 in which PARC technologies were presented to Xerox's senior management. He pushed for the commercialization of a more affordable Alto computer. Management ultimately decided to release a typewriter made by the Dallas based Xerox office systems division instead, which would have cost roughly the same amount to produce. Ellenby believed that the Dallas division resisted strongly to the release of a cheaper Alto because "they wouldn't make their numbers and therefore wouldn't get their bonuses ... as Ellenby gradually realized, the numbers were merely cannon fodder in a battle that was political to the core"[40].

Separation between PARC and Xerox Leads to Disjointed Inventions

PARC was set up in California, 3,000 miles away from Xerox headquarters in the East so that the research center would not only be close to major research universities focusing on technology, but also that it would be able to operate and innovate with as little corporate interference as possible. At the same time, however, the large geographical distance between the two, as well as Xerox's organizational complexity, engendered various cultural and organizational tensions and contributed to the sense of separation. There was insufficient integration between the two entities on an institutional level. At least for the first two decades of PARC's operation, there was no structured, rigorous system through which inventions from PARC could be evaluated and commercialized[41]. PARC scientist

Charles Geschke recalled that "on the few occasions we'd have McColough (Xerox's CEO between 1968 to 1982) come by it was like getting a state visit, you'd get fifteen minutes to pitch but there'd be no follow-through, no delegation to anyone who could understand what we were saying…"[42].

This separation did not help in terms of mutual understanding and trust. As chief scientist John Seely Brown recalled, "when managers tried to extend the knowledge created at PARC to the rest of the company, what had been intuitive among scientists working on the GUI proved almost unintelligible to the engineers who had to turn the ideas into marketable products. Insurmountable barriers of misunderstanding and then distrust developed between the communities. The scientists dismissed the engineers as copier-obsessed 'toner heads,' whereas the engineers found the scientists arrogant and unrealistic"[43].

The low level of coordination between Xerox and PARC was exacerbated by the complex organization structure of Xerox which led to high levels of bureaucracy and slow decision making. As a Xerox Spokesperson later noted: "we had layered complexity into a structure that laid on costs, slowed decision making and masked responsibility"[44]. Jacob Goldman, chief scientist at the founding of PARC, noted that with high structural complexity "there is, as a result, a loss of flexibility in the large organization and a compounding of overheads which translates itself into time delays in both the decision-making process and the introduction to market"[45]. Table 10.1 gives an outline of the above discussion.

Dominant logic at Xerox	*Business model* based on leasing high-end, proprietary copiers to corporate customers; and a pursuit of revenue growth and dominance of the copier market
	Focus on *core competence* of sales and after-sales service to safeguard revenues. The company's brand reputation in the copier market was a key resource
	Executive mindset focused on core business of copiers. There were corporate and individual performance targets, and risk aversion to technologies that were seen as unrelated to copiers
Org tensions	*Culture clash* due to goal misalignments between Xerox and PARC. Xerox focused on exploitation and PARC on exploration. Lack of mutual understanding between the two entities
	Rampant politics; internal competition for resources and active campaigning based on managerial and functional agendas
Disjointed inventions	*Structural separation* due to geographical distance between Xerox headquarters in the East and PARC in the West
	PARC followed its mission to invent office of the future and pursued *radical innovations* that did not have an explicit connection to the copier market
	Lack of integration mechanisms; there was no effective system for moving inventions to market; compounded by high organizational complexity and bureaucracy

Table 10.1. Dominant logic, organizational tensions and disjointed inventions at Xerox

As we can see in the Xerox and PARC story, the are many forces in established organizations that conspire to create inertia and shoot down efforts at innovation, flexibility adaptation, even when the best of intentions exist. These forces may lead to adverse consequence such as the Icarus paradox; the organization focuses so much on what made it successful to the exclusion of other potentially useful investments, to the point of ultimate failure. Xerox tried to invest in a Janus strategy where it could both exploit its copier business and simultaneously explore new technology and market options emerging through PARC and its other research labs. Yet, the organizational obstacles discussed in this chapter meant that this attempt failed. Competency traps are a mechanism that leads to such failure. As we will see in the next chapter, these traps have cognitive, organizational and behavioral dimensions that when acting together can create a deadly downward spiral.

Competency traps occur when an organization focuses
so much on what it does best, that it omits to invest in
new competencies that may be needed in the future.
When the competitive environment changes the
organization faces fatal risk or gradually becomes
irrelevant. The trap is that what the organization does
best is no longer what is needed for competitive success;
at the same time competitors' competencies may be
more aligned with market needs

11

Three Faces of Competency Traps

$\mathbf{X}$erox is a classic example of the Icarus paradox; a company that was market leader and focused so much on what it did best that it omitted to develop new avenues for competitiveness and performance. Its biggest strength, its copier-related competencies, became its downfall when the competitive environment shifted. Xerox had the right intentions; it wanted to explore other avenues. Consistent with a Janus approach, at the height of its success in the copier market, Xerox invested in PARC; a research subsidiary set up in 1970 that went on to invent groundbreaking technologies over the next 15 years. Apart from the laser printer however, most of these PARC-developed technologies were not commercialized by the company itself. The concept of competency traps can go a long way towards explaining what happened at Xerox.

A competency trap occurs when organizations develop experience and positive performance with particular procedures and routines, and then continue to use those procedures even when it is sub-optimal to do so, in a case of "maladaptive specialization"[1]. Competency traps have three underlying dimensions; cognitive, organizational and behavioral[2]. Together, these form powerful impediments to learning, innovation and change, including the pursuit of Janus strategies. We will elaborate on the Xerox case and other company examples as an illustration of these dimensions. In Xerox's case, its dominant logic is an example of the cognitive dimension of competency traps, disjointed inventions an example of the organizational dimension, and inter-unit organizational tensions an example of the behavioral dimension.

Cognitive Dimension of Competency Traps

The dominant logic of Xerox executives focused on a business model of leasing high-end, turnkey copier systems based on proprietary technology to large corporate customers[3]. Xerox's brand and reputation were key resources, supported by an extensive sales force and after sales service were seen as the company's core competencies. Executives concentrated their efforts on the core business of copiers to meet challenging company and individual performance targets. They were risk averse, unwilling to pursue new and uncertain businesses outside this core focus.

Dominant logic is enshrined in the "mental maps developed through experience in the core business"[4].

While it offers strategic guidance, it can also constrain business scope and lead to failure to exploit new opportunities. The dominant logic of Xerox at the time focused on how to accelerate printing by providing more reliable and efficient printers; yet most of PARC's inventions appropriately did not fit this logic. Xerox's past experience had too much influence on its choices for the future, in an instance of path dependency; "a firm's past experience conditions the alternatives management is able to perceive,"[5] particularly with respect to technological choices.

Polaroid's inertia and failure to adapt swiftly to digital photography is another case in point[6]. The company's dominant logic encompassed the razor/blade business model, where Polaroid was making the vast majority of its profits on the blade (the film) rather than the razor (the camera). The emergence of digital photography on the other hand required a business model focused on the cameras themselves (the razors), and involvement with consumer electronics and manufacturing of digital cameras rather than film. When digital cameras were commercially introduced in the 1990s Polaroid was unable to make this strategic shift swiftly and effectively enough, despite itself having conducted research in digital imaging technologies since the 1960s. Senior managers mistakenly assumed that customers would always want a paper printout and that Polaroid would use its chemical expertise to deliver high quality film and paper. Further, instant film had gross margins of over 65%[7], whereas consumer electronics including digital cameras were not nearly as profitable.

As with Polaroid, Xerox's business model was a razor/blade one, where the copiers were the razors and the number of copies made along with the after-sales and maintenance services Xerox provided were the blades. Xerox made its profits mainly on the copies and after sales services rather than the copiers. Xerox management's dominant logic was focused on defending, maintaining and refining that model rather than taking what they saw as uncertain and risky bets with low revenue potential on new technologies.

What strengthens the risk of competency traps is that organizations tend to move towards homogeneity, resting comfortably on mindsets and routines that support one preferable way of operating, and avoiding change that challenges this mindset and operating model[8]. In order to overcome myopic visions, leaders should develop processes for building both forward looking cognitive models as well as engage with backward-looking experiential learning[9]. This dual mode of thinking is one characteristic of Janus strategists.

Organizational Dimension of Competency Traps

Firms develop organizational routines, values and processes to support their core competency. The problem is that these routines and procedures may not be conducive to innovation and exploration, over time acting as competency traps when the environment shifts. One important way through which organizations innovate is through creating subsidiaries such as PARC. These subsidiaries often have their own routines, values and processes that are conducive to innovation; this is the reason they are initiated outside the core business in the first place.

The challenge then becomes how to effectively integrate innovative outputs within the corporate scope. This could be done by using innovations to support and strengthen the core business; by starting new businesses; or by spinning them off while retaining some equity interest; but allowing them the flexibility to compete and shift their business model as needed, rather than strangling them with the edicts and requirements of the corporation. Xerox's organizational paradigm was geared towards its dominant business, downplaying PARC inventions. According to John Seely Brown, former chief scientist at Xerox and PARC director, PARC was given the broad remit to pursue radical innovations and do basic research so that Xerox could become the "architect of innovation"; partly because incremental innovations were being pursued in Xerox's four other research laboratories. As a consequence, "there was a complete mismatch between Xerox's sales channels and many of the individual technologies that we were creating inside Xerox PARC"[10].

PARC's structural separation from Xerox was exacerbated by the vast geographical distance and the lack of integration mechanisms between the two. Xerox had no effective system for moving PARC's inventions to market, a situation compounded by Xerox's high levels of organizational complexity. An integration system was not needed to support Xerox's dominant logic and core business therefore the company did not develop one; leading to disjointed inventions, an instance of the organizational dimension of competency traps.

In setting up and funding PARC, Xerox overcame resource rigidity (the failure to reallocate resources to new capabilities or tasks), but crucially, not routine rigidity (the failure to change organizational processes) as a source of organizational inertia[11]. There was an absence of credible challenges to the dominant logic that would usher in the necessary unlearning and enable new learning to take place[12], which contributed to the persistence of routine rigidity. The lack of a structured model of discovery, incubation and acceleration to identify, nurture and successfully commercialize new technologies[13] compounded Xerox's inertial tendencies.

Behavioral Dimension of Competency Traps

As a company focuses on what it does best, it develops and encourages behaviors consistent with this pursuit. Innovative subsidiaries and more generally efforts at significant organization change or strategic re-orientation challenge such behaviors. The dominant paradigm seeks to fend off challenge and suppress attempts at innovation and change, a behavioral manifestation of competency traps. PARC posed a challenge to Xerox's dominant logic and established behaviors. Xerox leaders, with a focus on the core business, were not huge fans of PARC inventions (apart from the laser copier that enhanced the copier business). The culture clash between Xerox and PARC was characterised by goal misalignments, lack of mutual trust and understanding, and lack of willingness to experiment by Xerox executives. Rampant politicking took place via competition for resources and active campaigning based on individual and group agendas, with PARC often losing out in such political battles. Culture clash and politicking led to a high level of organizational tensions.

Around two decades after the establishment of PARC, Xerox created a more structured process for evaluating inventions and deciding whether to spin them off and how much equity to retain. The successful spinoffs however, used a very different business model than the one employed by Xerox. The more control Xerox retained by owning equity, keeping the spinoff in its annual budgetary cycle, and appointing its own CEO, the worse the spinoff performed; versus when the spinoff had more venture capitalists on its board and more strategic flexibility[14].

These interlinked cognitive, organizational and behavioral dimensions collectively led Xerox into a competency trap, where the company's core capabilities became core rigidities[15]. The market potential of PARC inventions was not recognised because of the already established dominant logic and associated organizational values and processes.

Leveraging Business Networks

One of the best ways to enhance the genetic pool of ideas, improve learning and adaptation and avoid falling in competency traps, is to actively participate in business networks. Through this process, firms can gain leading edge knowledge to support both exploitation of current resources and competencies, as well as exploration for new ones. As John Seely Brown noted, "knowledge is fundamentally changing from being contained within a corporation to being contained within ecosystems of partners[16]". NASA's commercial network model discussed previously for example is predicated on this assumption. For missions of immense complexity at risk of wicked problems, a single organization cannot have all the answers. A human mission to Mars for example will involve dimensions related to technical aspects of propulsion and flight, human health, particularly dealing with the effects of prolonged space exposure on the human body, psychological factors involved in carrying out a 2-year return trip to Mars in a small, enclosed craft, and survival technologies such as oxygen replenishment and water recycling. Effectively leveraging networks has become essential to finding answers to intractable challenges, and to continued competitiveness.

In this process of creating and participating in networks, openness and a learning mindset must prevail. This is not always the case however. The risk is that "stronger firms will avoid going out of their 'comfort zones' and eschew risky opportunities to leverage portfolio resources. Also, stronger firms will have a dismissive attitude toward external resources as they have become inwardly focused ... and prefer to stay on their own established technological trajectories"[17]. When a firm creates a separate innovation subsidiary, such as PARC, there is a danger of this subsidiary being seen as somehow "outside" the main organization, particularly if the dominant logic of the main organization is pervasive and unchallenged.

This was what happened at Xerox. Given the company's success in the copier business, executives over-valued the competencies associated with this business and undervalued PARC technologies perceived as unrelated, that nevertheless subsequently went on to shape the information technology industry. These technologies were seen as somehow "external" to the core business of copiers and marginal to Xerox's future competitive success despite the fact that they originated from within Xerox. Xerox as a corporation had invention capabilities, but it lacked *dynamic* capabilities; the ability of a corporation to sense opportunities and threats, seize opportunities, and reconfigure its operations as needed to enhance its competitiveness[18]. The lack of dynamic capabilities led to incumbent inertia[19], the organizational inflexibility arising from such conditions as asset lock-in, organizational routines and political dynamics.

Once competency traps set in, technologies with substantial promise can be treated as external to the organization even if they originate from within, mirroring the approach often taken by prominent and self-assured firms within alliance networks; an ultimately self-defeating strategy. Recognizing such organizational dysfunctions can enable a firm to purposefully pose challenges to its dominant logic, pay more attention to the potential of new technologies, and enhance its strategic options via active market experimentation with these technologies.

Eubulides of Miletus pondering one of the first versions of the "liar" paradox in the 4th century BC. Logical paradoxes such as these were so intractable that they pushed forward the study of logic. Yet, organizational paradoxes related to Janus strategy are less of the logical type, and more of the semantic and pragmatic types. Both of these can be addressed by re-framing contradictions and seeking synergistic solutions

12

Seeking Janus

In this book we explored how some leading organizations have pushed the envelope in terms of how they organize and how their leaders think strategically, seeking to transcend apparent contradictions and moving towards what we called Janus strategy. The business models, offerings, processes and accomplishments of these organizations speak for themselves. We used the six elements framework to highlight important strategic and operational choices these organizations made and to gain a more holistic understanding of how they pursued this type of strategy. The six elements are key ingredients of a recipe that necessarily allows and entails a lot of creativity. What particular aspects of these elements, and to what extent they are used, is up to the strategist.

As must be apparent by now there is no single way to accomplish Janus strategy. There are no easy solutions to strategic challenges, and if a solution was easy it would not afford sustainable advantage because it would be swiftly imitated by competitors. Rather, competitive advantage is built over time, by gradually building competencies that have certain key characteristics: They must be *valuable* to the customers, *rare* in the industry, and also *inimitable*, or at least hard to imitate by competitors. These competencies should be developed and employed within an organizational context that enables the company to gain value from them. In other words, the company should be properly *organized to exploit*[1] these competencies.

Our earlier discussion of Xerox highlights the importance of this last element, the ability to exploit particular competencies and resources. The invention competency that Xerox had in PARC was indeed *rare*, and also *inimitable*; or at least very hard to imitate by competitors at the time. PARC produced groundbreaking inventions that would be *valuable* to potential customers of the markets these inventions would open up. This potential however could only be fulfilled if an organization or leader were visionary enough to imagine, comprehend and then enact what these inventions could mean if introduced to market.

As it happens Apple founder Steve Jobs could do just that. He did in fact incorporate in his Macintosh computer many of the features he had seen at PARC when they demonstrated their Alto personal workstation. Jobs later mused: "If Xerox had known what it had and had taken advantage of its real opportunities, it could have been as big as IBM plus Microsoft plus Xerox combined - and the largest high- technology company in the world".[2]

For the various reasons we discussed in the chapters on Xerox and competency traps, the company was far from *organized to exploit* these inventions, the fourth key attribute of winning competencies. In fact, Xerox's focus on copiers and its reluctance to explore and commercialize what it saw as unrelated PARC inventions contributed to creating competency traps that the company could not escape from. The fourth piece of the puzzle was missing, and it cost Xerox billions of dollars in revenues, foregone market leadership, and greatness in the annals of corporate history.

The Six Elements and Their Contributions

The six elements represent or entail particular competencies that need to be built up over time in an interconnected and complementary way to support a firm's game plan. Together, they help an organization realize Janus strategy. The Table below indicates why each of the six elements is important to such a strategy and gives examples of how each element was employed in the various organizations we discussed.

The Six Elements	How element contributes to Janus strategy	Selected examples
Align but embrace paradox	Alignment improves efficiency and cost control (exploitation of current resources and competencies). Alignment can also foster inertia however through embedding a dominant logic, routines, sunk costs, and competency traps. Paradox, by drawing attention to both sides of a dilemma, fights inertia and promotes adaptability through its generative nature	Singapore airlines is highly aligned as shown by the ESCO model and the activity systems map (chapter 6). SIA also operates via the four paradoxes of cost-effective service excellence, simultaneous decentralized and centralized innovation, being a follower and a leader in service development, and employing standardization and personalization in service interactions (chapter 5). Toyota operates through several contradictions including having lean operations but delivering high quality, being both frugal and generous, both hierarchical but also granting autonomy (chapter 4)
Be a Janus strategist	Paradoxical thinking enables leaders to transcend binary choices and find solutions that synergize contradictory demands. Janus strategists focus both on competing in the present (exploitation) and also developing competencies for the future (exploration). They have an eye on both operations and the big picture, and challenge the status quo and dominant logics	Devi Shetty of Narayana Health challenged the dominant model of healthcare provision in India and created an organization able to consistently and sustainably offer complex healthcare at a fraction of competitors' costs and at higher quality levels (chapter 2). The NASA pirates believed that incumbent technology could not meet future demands and worked to create new technological capabilities while being pioneers in agile practices (chapter 9). Singapore Airlines executives aimed for both service excellence and high efficiency from the airline's founding to the present(chapter 6). Xerox executives are examples to the contrary (chapters 10 and 11)
Make dual strategic moves	Growth, alliances, investments, restructuring, and other strategic moves should aim towards synergizing competing goals such as efficiency and standardization, as well as innovation and personalization. Short-term return on capital calculations cannot capture such an orientation and may lead to ill-fated decisions if relied upon exclusively	Singapore Airlines trains its cabin crew for twice as long, incurring higher costs initially, but ensuring higher levels of service, cultural socialization, and commitment in the longer term (chapter 6). Apple makes several bite-sized acquisitions of young companies in upcoming domains to gain the technology it needs; this is both cheaper and faster than developing the tech itself (chapter 7). NASA's open innovation model and internal/external innovation provide fresh ideas and the advanced tech the agency needs for complex missions, faster and at lower cost than internal development (chapter 8)

The Six Elements	How element contributes to Janus strategy	Selected examples
Use tech to both exploit and explore	Technology investments are often made to optimize or standardize processes, without consideration of how technology can also raise quality, customize and open strategic options. Advance thinking in these terms increases the potential that technology can contribute to dual goals	Narayana Health uses tried and proven technology that is both reliable and cheaper than new and untested technology. Simultaneously, it invests in its own proprietary internal control information technology system to keep track of costs and increase the efficiency of operational processes, while sustaining quality levels (chapter 2). Singapore Airlines maintains a young fleet relative to competitors, which is both cheaper to operate and maintain, and offers enhanced customer experience levels (chapter 6). Apple's iOs system is used across its devices, providing both efficiencies in development and maintenance of the software, as well as enhanced customer experience via interconnectivity of devices; in turn supporting Apple's ecosystem strategy (chapter 7)
Design agile organizat ion	Agility aims to enhance adaptability and innovation, as well as reduce cost through lean processes and practices. Its philosophy is aligned with Janus strategy, in particular finding ways to transcend competing demands	NASA has exhibited strategic agility by evolving its business model, capabilities and practices from the hierarchical model to the inter-governmental partnership model, and then to the commercial network model (chapter 8). NASA pirates developed and used agile practices and were true agile pioneers, well before agility became a fashion (chapter 9). Apple's corporate structure is functionally oriented, flat and lean, despite the huge size of the company (chapter 7). Xerox is an example to the contrary, a company that fell in its own competency traps and that lacked the agility to commercialize most of the groundbreaking inventions of its own research laboratory, PARC (chapters 10 and 11)
Leverage business networks	Effective inter-organizational networks enable transfer of learning, optimization, and support business models that take advantage of comparative advantage. An organization can focus on what it can do best, or what can grant it competitive advantage, and outsource other necessary inputs while also employ networks to remain on the leading edge	Narayana Health works with networks of local suppliers for quality inputs at lower cost. In this way it ensures reliability of the supply chain, high quality levels, and cost control. It owns and operates a network of 47 healthcare facilities, allowing it achieve economies as well as transfer of learning (chapter 2). Apple is a network organization, outsourcing most inputs and retaining control of functions where it can add most value; research & development, design, marketing, and distribution via the Apple stores. This provides both immense efficiency to Apple given its negotiating power, as well as the ability to focus on value-added, exploration-oriented activities (chapter 7). NASA's commercial network model embeds the agency within networks of partners and enables the efficient acquisition, and seeding, of mission-relevant knowledge and technology wherever it is based to accomplish missions of ever-increasing complexity (chapter 8)

Table 12.1. How the six elements contribute to Janus strategy

Janusian Thinking by Organizational Leaders

The central element in the six elements figure is the Janus strategist who orchestrates everything else. I worded this in the singular form for ease of reference, but it could just as easily be a number of strategists, whether or not they are formally labeled as such. Individuals who can see the big picture in relation to current operational demands and who can conceive of the trends leading into the future and their operational implications, deserve to be called strategists whether or not the organization recognizes them as such. So the Janus strategist could be a particular leader, such as Narayana Health's founder Devi Shetty or Steve Jobs of Apple. It could be a group of executives, such as the leaders of Singapore Airlines. Or it could be groups of individuals dispersed at different parts of the organization, such as the NASA pirates.

In this final chapter, it is worth examining in more detail the Janus strategist and the thought processes that may be involved. We started the book by discussing Harvard psychiatrist Albert Rothenberg's research[3] on Janusian thinking. Rothenberg identified four phases of the creative process of Nobel prize-winning scientists: the motivation to create or innovate; separation or deviation from the dominant perspectives; bringing together of opposites when contemplating challenges of the field; and finally creating theory where the insights are stated in a more linear, causal, or propositional way.

If we relate these four phases to organizational leaders who we identified as Janus strategists, we see similar themes. First, they are motivated to create something different, to push the envelope, because they feel that a new process, offering, or way of organizing is needed to address particular challenges. This desire to create something new was marked in the leaders of several of the organizations we discussed; Dr Devi Shetty at Narayana, the leadership team of Singapore Airlines, Steve Jobs at Apple, the pirates at NASA.

Second, in every one of these examples, these leaders' thinking deviated from the dominant perceptions and solutions. Dr Shetty conceived of and created a new business model in a notoriously inertial sector, healthcare. At the founding of the airline, Singapore Airlines leaders aimed for both service excellence and intense internal efficiency, an approach that was unique at that point in the aviation industry. Steve Jobs, through Apple, brought user-friendly personal computing to the masses at a time when using a computer had been a complex and frustrating undertaking by people who were not scientists or engineers. Jobs then restructured the music industry through the iPod and introduced the iPhone that blurred industry boundaries through technology convergence. The NASA pirates aimed to develop mission control technology that would shift the agency's reliance from the established mainframe model to the new approach of distributed computing.

Third, all these leaders sought to transcend binary tensions and find solutions that were both/and rather than either/or. As we saw in earlier discussions, Narayana Health delivers high quality healthcare at a fraction of the cost of not just Western but also other local Indian health facilities. Singapore Airlines operates along four paradoxes with the primary one being cost effective service excellence. Apple is a high-end competitor recognized for world class innovation, yet also operates at a surprising level of efficiency. The NASA pirates delivered a system that had both higher and expanded functionality; yet was also considerably cheaper to operate than the prior system.

Rothenberg's fourth element was the creation of theory based on the insights gained. Nobel prize-winning scientists eventually had to express their emergent and often unexpected paradoxical insights in a more linear, causal, testable format. Applying the analogy to organizational leaders, we can see this as corresponding to the development of particular business models that encompass those insights. We used the six elements to explore various aspects of the business models of Narayana Health, Singapore Airlines, Apple, and NASA in earlier chapters. The six elements highlight the applied choices that these Janus strategists made to operationalize their prior insights on what could lead their organizations to competitive success. Choosing a course of action has opportunity costs in terms of funds, management time, and other resources. Yet a particular course of action does not necessarily imply binary, either/or logic if it is guided by deeper insights that seek to synergize competing tensions and accomplish dual outcomes.

Integrative Strategic Thinking

Janus strategists are holistic, integrative thinkers. In the design of higher education in Ancient Greece from around 420BC onwards, the domains of arts and sciences were brought together to inculcate more subtle and holistic ways of thinking and understanding the world. Classical education encompassed dialectic, music, gymnastics, astronomy and mathematics.

More recently, psychologists and educators explicitly investigated the idea of integrative thinking. One useful perspective is that such thinking consists of three components: "1. *Complexity*: the ability to recognize complex relationships, particularly when dealing with ambiguous, contradictory and incomplete information. 2. *Adaptability*: an ability to approach problems in new ways when traditional or conventional methods are ineffective and to be able to recognize that new approaches are needed. 3. *Open-mindedness*: a willingness to see another's viewpoint, thereby showing openness to interpretations which differ from one's own"[4].

This sounds very much like the type of thinking that an effective strategist might do. Strategic challenges reside very much within the domain of the ambiguous, complex and contradictory. The map (mental model), must be able to perceive the subtleties and key aspects of the territory (strategic challenges), so as to satisfy the *complexity* element above. Conventional solutions may help an organization survive, but only going beyond convention in their offerings, business models or processes can organizations reach greatness or at least competitive advantage and to satisfy the *adaptability* element above. Finally, *open-mindedness* is one of the best ways to defend against a variety of cognitive biases that pull towards habitual solutions and reinforce existing mental maps rather than extend or reframe mental maps to deal with new kinds of challenges.

Structured, rational frameworks have been suggested to enable integrative thinking, such as a cascade decision process starting from identifying the salient parts of a challenge, recognizing the causality among these elements in leaders' mental models, re-arranging causal relationships towards desired outcomes, and finally making the best decision possible given the prior analysis[5]. Such frameworks and tools are helpful for training and development, and for sensitizing leaders to the importance of challenging one's existing mental maps. Yet, as Rothenberg and others showed, in practice the creative process of gaining ingenious ideas that open new vistas, the sort of thinking that is needed to conceive of Janus strategies, is less structured and even partly unconscious.

Generative Role of the Unconscious

Rothenberg found that the crux of Janusian thinking, the bringing together of opposites in his phase three, occurs most often as a flash of insight, brought about seemingly by chance via unconscious processes. But such a process is not completely random in its existence; it draws on ongoing deep engagement with, and intimate knowledge of, the field: "The truly creative person knows his field well and also knows which widely held notions, beliefs, and 'facts' are important and susceptible to opposition or contradiction on some level. It is this type of knowledge, a knowledge which may come into play after the creator hits on an integrated opposition by chance, unconscious determination, or other factors, which makes the Janusian thought meaningful and, in fact, valuable"[6].

Jacques Hadamard, a distinguished French mathematician, wanted to understand what he called the "psychology of invention" in mathematics. He reflected on his own thought processes, interviewed other mathematicians, and also sent out a survey inquiring on these themes. He noted that "the unconscious has the important property of being manifold; several and probably many things can and do occur in it simultaneously. ... this multiplicity of the unconscious enables it to carry out a work of synthesis"[7]. Creativity theorist Arthur Koestler concurred with Hadamard's findings that "the role of strictly rational and verbal processes in scientific discovery has been vastly over-estimated[8]".

Hadamard received a reply to his survey that conveyed "information of capital interest"[9] as he put it, since it described Albert Einstein's effort to reflect on his thought processes. Einstein wrote: "The words or the language, as they are written or spoken, do not seem to play any role in my mechanism of thought. The psychical entities which seem to serve as elements in thought are certain signs and more or less clear images which can be 'voluntarily' reproduced and combined. There is, of course, a certain connection between those elements and relevant logical concepts. It is also clear that the desire to arrive finally at logically connected concepts is the emotional basis of this rather vague play with the above mentioned elements. But taken from a psychological viewpoint, this combinatory play seems to be the essential feature in productive thought—before there is any connection with logical construction in words or other kinds of signs which can be communicated to others. The above mentioned elements are, in my case, of visual and some of muscular type. Conventional words or other signs have to be sought for laboriously only in a secondary stage, when the mentioned associative play is sufficiently established and can be reproduced at will.

According to what has been said, the play with the mentioned elements is aimed to be analogous to certain logical connections one is searching for. ... In a stage when words intervene at all, they are, in my case, purely auditive, but they interfere only in a secondary stage as already mentioned"[10].

Einstein's "combinatory play" of images was fundamental to his theorizing and gaining insights. What he is describing here is the playground for Rothenberg's phase three, where contradictory ideas can be potentially brought together; and phase four, "the desire to arrive finally at logically connected concepts" when "conventional words or other signs have to be sought for laboriously only in a secondary stage". Even though the play Einstein describes could be somehow intentional and guided (Einstein put "voluntarily" in quotation marks), several of his defining ideas appeared rather unexpectedly during such "associative play". One example that led to his theory of relativity is his realization that when a man is falling in a vacuum, from their perspective they are stationary since whatever objects they release would fall at the same rate. So the man can be falling and stationary at the same time depending on where the observer is located[11].

Mozart described in a letter how he got ideas for his melodies. He had no conscious control of when musical compositions would come to him. When they did, he did not know where they came from. But he did retain and elaborate those he liked: "When I feel well disposed, in good humour and given up to myself altogether, when I am alone and have a calm and satisfied mind, as, for instance, when I am travelling in a good carriage, or taking a stroll after a good meal, or in bed at night without being asleep, then it is that ideas come to me and throng into my mind. Those that please me, I retain, and even hum; at least, so others have told me. It seems to me impossible to say whence they come to me and how they arrive; what is certain is that I cannot make them come when I wish"[12].

It is clear that the unconscious is active, sometimes sends ideas to the conscious mind, these ideas may be conveyed in symbolic terms, and they can be generative. This is so for scientists, artists, individuals at large, and it is no different for strategists. Hadamard's early realizations anticipate later attention to how the unconscious can work on particular challenges unbeknownst to the conscious mind, and then suggest solutions that seem to the conscious mind to appear out of the blue[13].

Child prodigies and mathematical savants for example seem to unconsciously employ complex, multi-step algorithms to accomplish calculating feats only otherwise accomplished by computers. After reflection, they may sometimes be able to consciously explain some part of how they accomplish their cognitive feats if others ask them to. Most often however they do not try to explain analytically how they do it, and they don't need to; conscious explanation is not necessary for their abilities to operate. Psychologists have termed "incubation effects" the unconscious processes that occur when a problem is temporarily set aside by the conscious mind, until efforts to solve it begin again[14]. During this time the unconscious may provide new perspectives on the problem, different, previously unrecognized connections between concepts, or some kind of reframing that may help lead to a novel solution.

Toward Janusian Thinking

Given all we discussed, including the role of paradox and the unconscious, Janusian thinking is more of a cognitive orientation and a thought practice rather than a tool or analytical approach that can be used at will. Of course, particular tools or methods may help individuals appreciate more about what such thinking involves, but these tools most likely cannot routinely reproduce such thinking. There is no tool, method or process that can be handed out to unfailingly produce Janusian thinking. That would be too easy and ultimately worthless for competitive advantage, since it could be easily employed by everyone. Paradigm-shifting discoveries usually do not arise as a result of any structured tools but emerge as sparks of paradoxical insight that appears happenstance but is informed and enabled by prior intention, knowledge and capability. After the insights occur, they are expressed in a more linear form and subjected to the structured reasoning and tools of science; Rothenberg's stages three and four, and as Einstein also noted.

What leaders can do is to develop their thinking practices over time. They can set a conscious intention and make a habit of reflecting on strategic challenges in non-binary terms, seeking to go beyond obvious choices. They can consciously and routinely try to re-frame issues so they can be examined from a variety of angles; and sidestep the most common cognitive biases. They can consciously explore instances of how other organizations, groups, or individuals have gained insights and accomplished synergizing of competing pressures that is characteristic of Janus strategy; and see what may be learned.

To create a supportive organizational context, it is important to institute practices that are intended to reduce the impact of destructive cognitive biases such as groupthink[15] and the inertia of tradition, by introducing real conversations and diversity of views. Group dynamics and decision-making tools that can foster debate, even juxtaposition of opposing views such as thesis-antithesis-synthesis[16] and devil's advocate[17] can be very helpful. So can processes that encourage storytelling and sensemaking, such as construction, interpretation and debate of physical analogues of strategic challenges[18]. Such techniques can not only lead to better decisions but can also strengthen individuals' commitment to the decisions once they are reached[19].

Insights from this type of thinking may not just relate to the overall gameplan of the organization, but also to which of the six elements to emphasize given the organization's situation, what aspects of these elements, and how to combine them to realize Janus strategies. We explored in this book the various ways through which organizations such as Narayana Health, Toyota, Singapore Airlines, Apple, and NASA used these elements to build strategies that have led to outperformance and sustainable advantage. The palette is there; now it's up to you, as strategist, how to use it to lead your own organization.

Mozart was one of several geniuses who reported that they could not control when or how inspiration and creative ideas came. In this case, melodies for new compositions came unexpectedly into Mozart's mind. When they did, he did not know where they came from. But he hummed them and remembered them. The unconscious can be generative when properly nurtured. Flashes of insight may emerge unexpectedly and may give solutions to, or new frames for seeing and dealing with intractable challenges

Glossary of Key Terms

Agility

Strategic agility is the ability of an organization to shift business models over time so it can sustain its competitiveness. This includes effective use of inter-organizational networks and appropriate balancing of speed and stability. *Organizational* agility is the ability to adapt, experiment, reallocate resources as needed, and unlearn past routines that no longer deliver value. *Leadership* agility is the ability of leaders to sense environmental signals, evaluate the implications, and take initiative to drive the organization forward

Alignment

Strategic alignment involves mutual consistency and fit among four elements: Environment, Strategy, Competencies and Organization. External alignment refers to consistency and fit between strategy and environment; internal alignment refers to consistency and fit between strategy, competencies and organization. See also ESCO model

Ambidexterity

As an analogy from an individual's capability to have equal dexterity in both hands, this term refers to the capability of an organization to balance competing tensions such as exploitation of current resources and competencies while simultaneously exploring for new ones; and to work effectively with contradictions and paradoxes (see also Contradiction and Paradox). Ambidexterity supports the implementation of Janus Strategy

Competency trap

Competency traps occur when organizations focus single-mindedly on competencies that have led to success, and omit to invest in, and develop, additional competencies that may be needed in future. In ambidexterity terms, competency traps result from high focus on exploitation and little or no focus on exploration (see also Ambidexterity). Competency traps have cognitive, organizational and behavioral dimensions

Contradiction

A contradiction exists when opposing or inconsistent elements are brought together. Contradictions could be logical, semantic, cognitive and/or organizational. See also Paradox

Dominant logic

Refers to management teams' paradigm about their market, their company's competencies, and more broadly about how they should play the competitive game. Dominant logic provides strategic guidance, but also often acts as a blinder to seeing alternative strategic choices

ESCO model

ESCO is a strategic alignment model suggesting that the four elements of Environment, Strategy, Competencies and Organization should be mutually consistent and supportive for alignment to be accomplished. The model is explained in detail in Heracleous & Werres, 2016, On the road to disaster: Strategic misalignments and corporate failure, Long Range Planning

Icarus paradox

Derives from the mythological story of Icarus escaping Crete with his father Daedalus by using wings held together with wax. Icarus ignored warnings not to fly too close to the sun, which melted the wax and sent him plunging to his death. The term refers to what is one's greatest strength becoming their biggest weakness because they focus too much on it. Competency traps lead to the Icarus Paradox (See also Competency traps)

Janus

The Roman god of beginnings and endings, gateways and transitions. He is portrayed as having two, four or six heads facing in opposite directions, to portray his dual or multiple nature in terms of simultaneously bringing together opposites and contradictions

Janus strategy

A strategy that involves synergizing competing tensions, and developing two or more capabilities that have traditionally been considered distinct and incompatible (such as service excellence at budget level cost, or high levels of innovation as well as intense efficiency). In terms of traditional strategy vocabulary, Janus strategy combines differentiation and cost leadership not just temporarily but in the longer term, something considered impossible by strategic orthodoxy

Janus strategist

A strategist who can simultaneously hold contradictory ideas in their mind (such as the two poles of a dilemma or a paradox), who does not seek to simplify and collapse these ideas to either/or binary interpretations, and who strives for novel solutions that transcend contradictions and the constraints imposed by any single idea. This mindset, together with appropriate organizational arrangements relating to the six elements, can enable Janus Strategy to be conceptualized and implemented

Paradox

A paradox is created when two propositions that can individually be valid, form a logical impossibility when juxtaposed. See also Contradiction

Six elements

The six inter-related operational and strategic elements that together enable the realization of Janus strategy. They are as follows: be a Janus strategist, align but embrace paradox, make dual strategic moves, use technology to both exploit and explore, design agile organization, and leverage business networks

About the Author

Loizos Heracleous is Professor of Strategy and Organization at Warwick Business School, and Associate Fellow at Said Business School and Green Templeton College at Oxford University. He earned his PhD from the University of Cambridge and received a Higher Doctorate (DSc) from the University of Warwick for lifetime contributions to his field. He researches and teaches about strategy, organization change and development, and corporate governance. His research has been published in 10 books and over 80 research papers, in journals that include the *Academy of Management Journal, Academy of Management Review, Strategic Management Journal, MIS Quarterly, Harvard Business Review* and *MIT Sloan Management Review*. His work has been honored over the years by four Awards from the US Academy of Management and by three awards from Emerald. He is a recipient of the *Douglas McGregor Award* from the *Journal of Applied Behavioral Science* and has served on the editorial boards of several leading journals. He has worked with senior leaders at several blue-chip corporations and agencies and is regularly quoted in business media. More information about Loizos' work can be found at www.heracleous.org and at his Twitter feed @Strategizing.

Endnotes

Prologue

[1] Hampden-Turner, C. 1990. Charting the corporate mind. Oxford: Blackwell.

[2] Porter, M. E. 1980. Competitive strategy: Techniques for analysing industries and competitors. NY: Free Press.

[3] Heracleous, L. & Wirtz, J. 2010. Singapore Airlines' balancing act. Harvard Business Review, July-August: 145-149.

[4] Heracleous, L. 2013. Quantum strategy at Apple Inc. Organizational Dynamics, 42: 92-99.

[5] Duncan, R. B. 1976. The ambidextrous organization: Designing dual structures for innovation. In Kilman, R. H., Pondy, L. R. & Slevin, D. P. (Eds.). The management of organization design: Strategies and implementation. NY: North-Holland: 167-188.

[6] Bartlet, C. A. & Ghoshal, S. 1988. Organizing for worldwide effectiveness: The transnational solution. California Management Review, 31(1): 54-74.

[7] March, J. G. 1991. Exploration and exploitation in organizational learning. Organization Science, 2: 71-87.

[8] Abell, D. F. 1999. Competing today while preparing for tomorrow. MIT Sloan Management Review, 40(3): 73-81.

[9] Markides, C. & Charitou, C. D. 2004. Competing with dual business models. Academy of Management Perspectives, 18(3):22-36.

[10] Hayakawa, S. I. 1947. Language in action. NY: Harcourt, Brace & Co.

1. Be like Janus

[1] Ovid, 1921. Metamorphoses. Translated by F. J. Miller, Cambridge, MA: Harvard University Press. Quote from book VIII, pp. 421, 423.

[2] Miller, D. 1992. The Icarus paradox: How exceptional companies bring about their own downfall. Business Horizons, Jan/Feb: 24-35.

[3] Heracleous, L., Papachroni, A., Andriopoulos, C. & Gotsi, M. 2017. Structural ambidexterity and competency traps: Insights from Xerox PARC. Technological Forecasting and Social Change, 117: 327-338. See also Robson, D. 2020. How to avoid the "competency trap". BBC Worklife, 9 June. Available at: https://www.bbc.com/worklife/article/20200608-what-is-the-competency-trap

[4] Abell, D. F. 1999, Competing for today while preparing for tomorrow, Sloan Management Review, Spring, 73-81.

[5] March, J. G. 1991, Exploration and exploitation in organizational learning, Organization Science, 2: 71-86.

[6] Taylor, R. 2000. Watching the skies. Janus, auspication, and the shrine in the Roman forum. Memoirs of the American Academy in Rome, 45: 1-40.

[7] See e.g. Bartunek, J. 1988. The dynamics of personal and organizational reframing. In Quinn, R. E. & Cameron, K. S. (Eds.). Paradox and transformation: Toward a theory of change in organization and management. Cambridge, MA: Ballinger: 137-162; Tushman, M. L., Smith, W. K. & Binns, A. 2011. The ambidextrous CEO. Harvard Business Review, June, 74-80; Lavine, M. 2014. Paradoxical leadership and the competing values framework. Journal of Applied Behavioral Science, 50: 189-205; Papachroni, A. & Heracleous, L. 2020. Ambidexterity as practice: Individual

ambidexterity though paradoxical practices. Journal of Applied Behavioral Science, 56.

[8] Davenport, C. 2017. Who was Janus, the Roman god of beginnings and endings? The Conversation, 31 December. Available at: https://theconversation.com/who-was-janus-the-roman-god-of-beginnings-and-endings-86853

[9] Wasson, D. L. 2015. Janus. Ancient History Encyclopedia. Available at: https://www.ancient.eu/Janus/

[10] Heraclitus, fragment LIX. In Patrick, G. T. W. 1889. The fragments of the work of Heraclitus of Ephesus on Nature. Baltimore: N Murray. Quote is from page 99.

[11] Stevenson, R. L. 1904. The strange case of Dr Jekyll and Mr Hyde. New York: Scott-Thaw Company. Quote is from page 152.

[12] Barnum, P. T. 1855. The life of P. T. Barnum. Written by himself. New York: Redfield. Quote is from page 10.

[13] Dickson, D. H. & Kelly, I. W. 1985. The "Barnum effect" in personality assessment: A review of the literature. Psychological Reports, 57: 367-382.

[14] See for example the meta-analysis by Junni, P., Sarala, R. M., Taras, V. & Tarba, S. Y. 2013. Organizational ambidexterity and performance. A meta-analysis. Academy of Management Perspectives, 27(4): 299-312.

[15] Rothenberg, A. 1996. The Janusian process of scientific creativity. Creativity Research Journal, 9: 207-231. Rothenberg, A. 2015. Flight from wonder: An investigation of scientific creativity. Oxford: Oxford University Press.

[16] Rothenberg, A. 1971. The process of Janusian thinking in creativity. Archives of General Psychiatry, 24: 195-205. Quote from p. 195.

[17] Rothenberg, A. 1971. The process of Janusian thinking in creativity. Archives of General Psychiatry, 24: 195-205. Quotes from p. 196.

[18] The descriptions of Janusian thinking by Darwin, Einstein and Bohr draw from Rothenberg (1996) and (2015).

[19] Einstein, A. 1920. Fundamental ideas and methods of the theory of relativity, presented in their development. Einstein Archives, Institute for Advanced Study, Princeton, New Jersey. Availlable at: https://einsteinpapers.press.princeton.edu/vol7-trans/129

[20] Bohr, N. 1928.The quantum postulate and the recent development of atomic theory. Supplement to Nature, April 14, 580-590. Quote from p. 581.

[21] Rothenberg, A. 1996. The Janusian process of scientific creativity. Creativity Research Journal, 9: 207-231. Rothenberg, A. 2015. Flight from wonder: An investigation of scientific creativity. Oxford: Oxford University Press.

[22] Kuhn, T. S. 1962. The structure of scientific revolutions. Chicago: University of Chicago Press.

[23] Koestler, A. 1964. The act of creation. London: Hutchinson. See also Koestler, A. 1967. The three domains of creativity. In Bugental, J. F. T. (Ed.), Challenges of humanistic psychology. NY: McGraw-Hill, pp. 31-40. Quotes are from pages 31-32.

[24] The generative role of the unconscious has been recognized by several theorists including Rothenberg and informed by accounts of several scientists and artists. We will take up this topic in more detail in the final chapter.

[25] Rothenberg, A. 1996. The Janusian process of scientific creativity. Creativity Research Journal, 9: 207-231. Quote from p. 219.

2. Toward Janus strategy

[1] These medical statistics are from Narayana Health's Annual Report 2018-2019, available at: https://www.narayanahealth.org/sites/default/files/downlo ad/annual-reports/Annual_Report_2018_19.pdf

[2] More details about Narayana Hospital and Dr Shetty can be found in Bruce, K. & Heracleous, L. 2015, Narayana Health: Bringing quality healthcare to the masses, The Case Center, Case 315-202-1; and in Heracleous, L. & Bruce, K. 2015, Narayana Health Case Teaching Notes, The Case Center, 315-202-8.

[3] Narayana Health Investor Presentation, January 2020.

[4] Altstedter, A., 2019, The world's cheapest hospital has to get even cheaper, Bloomberg Businessweek, 26 March. Available at: https://www.bloomberg.com/news/features/2019-03-26/the-world-s-cheapest-hospital-has-to-get-even-cheaper

[5] Information from: Bruce, K. & Heracleous, L. 2015, Narayana Health: Bringing quality healthcare to the masses, The Case Center, Case 315-202-1; and in Heracleous, L. & Bruce, K. 2015, Narayana Health Case Teaching Notes, The Case Center, 315-202-8; Altstedter, A., 2019, The world's cheapest hospital has to get even cheaper, Bloomberg Businessweek, 26 March. Available at: https://www.bloomberg.com/news/features/2019-03-26/the-world-s-cheapest-hospital-has-to-get-even-cheaper; Mohan, R. 2018. Smart surgery and low-cost healthcare in India. Think:Act, Roland Berger, available at: https://www.rolandberger.com/en/Point-of-View/Smart-surgery-and-low-cost-health-care-in-India.html

[6] Kothandaraman, P. & Mookerjee, S. 2008, Healthcare for all: Narayana Hrudayalaya, Bangalore, Available from:

http://growinginclusivemarkets.org/media/cases/India_Na rayana_Summary.pdf

[7] Devan, J., Klusas, M. B., Ruefli, T. W.2007. The elusive goal of corporate outperformance. McKinsey Quarterly, May: 1-4.

[8] Haanaes, K., Reeves, M. & Wurlod, J. 2018. The 2% company. Boston Consulting Group. Available at: https://www.bcg.com/en-gb/publications/2018/2-percent-company

[9] Michael Porter advanced his influential ideas on generic strategies and their implementation, as well as the need to make a clear choice among strategies, in Competitive strategy (Free Press, 1980) and Competitive advantage: Creating and sustaining superior performance (Free Press, 1985).

[10] For more information on Michael Porter's position and on the history of the strategy field see Heracleous, L. 2003. Strategy and organization: Realizing strategic management. Cambridge: Cambridge University Press, chapter 1.

[11] Heracleous, L. & Wirtz, J. 2010. Singapore Airlines' balancing act. Harvard Business Review, July-August: 145-149.

[12] Heracleous, L. 2013. Quantum strategy at Apple Inc. Organizational Dynamics, 42: 92-99.

[13] These companies have been labeled "Chinese dragons". See Williamson, P. J., 2010, Cost innovation: Preparing for a "value for money" revolution, Long Range Planning, 43: 343-353.

[14] Heracleous, L., 2013, Quantum Strategy at Apple Inc, Organizational Dynamics, 42, 92-99; Heracleous, L., 2013, What do Apple and Singapore Airlines have in common? Quantum strategy, Bloomberg Business, Available at http://www.bloomberg.com/bw/articles/2013-07-31/what-

do-apple-and-singapore-airlines-have-in-common-quantum-strategy; Heracleous, L., 2009, Quantum strategies and organizational resilience, Warwick Business School, Academic Update Review, 12 September, https://www.wbs.ac.uk/alumni/news/2009/10/09/Academic/Update/review

[15] The growing potential of quantum computing. Interview of Vern Brownell, CEO of C-Wave Systems, McKinsey Global Institute, February 2016. See also Eisert, J., Wilkens, M. & Lewenstein, M., 1999, Quantum games and quantum strategies, Physical Review Letters, 83, 3077-3080. Eisert et al. found that quantum strategies outperform classical strategies in the game of Prisoners' Dilemma.

[16] Reeves, M. Bergman, R., Gourevitch, A. & Ortiz, M., 2016, Forks in the road: Navigating industry disruption, Boston Consulting Group, www.bcgperspectives.com, p. 1.

[17] March, J. G. 1991, Exploration and exploitation in organizational learning, Organization Science, 2: 71-86.

[18] Abell, D. F. 1999, Competing for today while preparing for tomorrow, Sloan Management Review, Spring, 73-81.

3. The six elements

[1] Parts of the discussion in this chapter draw from Heracleous, L. 2013, Quantum Strategy at Apple Inc, Organizational Dynamics, 42, 92-99.

[2] Porter, M. E. 1985. Competitive advantage: Creating and sustaining superior performance. NY: Free Press, pp. 11-12.

[3] Porter, M. E. 1985. Competitive advantage: Creating and sustaining superior performance. NY: Free Press, pp. 19-20.

[4] Porter, M. E. 1985. Competitive advantage: Creating and sustaining superior performance. NY: Free Press p. 20.

[5] For further details of Danny Miller's research on generic

strategies and whether firms could combine features of these strategies, see Miller, D. 1988, Relating Porter's business strategies to environment and structure: Analysis and performance implications, Academy of Management Journal, 31: 280-308; Miller, D. and Friesen, P. H. 1986a, Porter's (1980) generic strategies and performance: An empirical examination with American data, Part I: Testing Porter. Organization Studies, 7: 37-55; and Miller, D. and Friesen, P. H. 1986b, Porter's (1980) generic strategies and performance: An empirical examination with American data, Part II: Performance implications, Organization Studies, 7: 255-261.

6 Hill, C. W. L. 1988. Differentiation versus low cost or differentiation and low cost: A contingency framework. Academy of Management Review, 13: 401-412.

7 Tushman and O'Reilly advanced their ideas on structural ambidexterity in Tushman, M. L. and O'Reilly, C. A. 1996, Ambidextrous organizations: Managing evolutionary and revolutionary change, California Management Review, 38 (4): 8–30; and in O'Reilly, C. A. and Tushman, M. L. 2004, The ambidextrous organization, Harvard Business Review, April: 2-9.

8 Bartunek, J. 1988. The dynamics of personal and organizational reframing. In Quinn, R. E. & Cameron, K. S. (Eds.). Paradox and transformation: Toward a theory of change in organization and management. Cambridge, MA: Ballinger: 137-162; Tushman, M. L., Smith, W. K. & Binns, A. 2011. The ambidextrous CEO. Harvard Business Review, June, 74-80.

9 Heracleous, L., Papachroni, A., Andriopoulos, C. & Gotsi, M. 2017. Structural ambidexterity and competency traps: Insights from Xerox PARC. Technological Forecasting and Social Change, 117: 327-338.

[10] Markides and Charitou have discussed their views on dual business models in Markides, C. and Charitou, C. D. 2004. Competing with dual business models: A contingency approach. Academy of Management Executive, 18(3): 22-36.

[11] E.g. see Romanelli, E., & Tushman, M. L. 1994. Organizational transformation as punctuated equilibrium: An empirical test. Academy of Management Journal, 37: 1141–1666; and Siggelkow, N., & Levinthal, D. A. 2003. Temporarily divide to conquer: Centralized, decentralized, and reintegrated organizational approaches to exploration and adaptation. Organization Science, 14: 650-669.

[12] As Henry Mintzberg suggested that strategy can be seen as a pattern in a stream of actions. See Mintzberg, H. 1978. Patterns in strategy formation. Management Science, 24: 934-948.

[13] See Bartlett, C. A. & Wozny, M. 2005. GE's two-decade transformation: Jack Welch's leadership. Harvard Business School Case 9-399-150.

[14] See e.g. Stadler, C., Rajwani, T., Karaba, F. 2014. Solutions to the exploration/exploitation dilemma: Networks as a new level of analysis. International Journal of Management Reviews, 16: 172-193; and Kauppila, O.P. 2010. Creating ambidexterity by integrating and balancing structurally separate interorganizational partnerships. Strategic Organization, 8: 283-312.

[15] Birkinshaw and Gibson advanced their arguments on contextual ambidexterity in Birkinshaw, J. and Gibson, C. 2004. Building ambidexterity into an organization, MIT Sloan Management Review, Summer: 47-55; and in Gibson, C. and Birkinshaw, J. 2004. The antecedents, consequences, and mediating role of organizational ambidexterity, Academy of Management Journal, 47: 209-226.

[16] Papachroni, A., Heracleous, L. & Paroutis, S. 2016. In pursuit of ambidexterity: Managerial reactions to innovation-efficiency tensions. Human Relations, 69: 1791-1822.

[17] The Boston Consulting Group referred to these four approaches as separation, switching, external ecosystem and self-organizing. See Reeves, M., Haanaes, K., Hollingsworth, J. & Scognamiglio, F. 2013. Ambidexterity: The art of thriving in complex environments. Boston Consulting Group, February 19. Available at: https://www.bcg.com/publications/2013/strategy-growth-ambidexterity-art-thriving-complex-environments. These four approaches are also discussed in chapter 7 of Reeves, M., Haanaes, K. & Sinha, J. 2015. Your strategy needs a strategy: How to choose and execute the right approach. Boston, MA: Harvard Business Review Press.

[18] Hayakawa, S. I. 1947. Language in action. NY: Harcourt, Brace & Co.

[19] Reeves, M. & Levin, S. 2017. Think biologically: Messy management for a complex world. Boston Consulting Group, July 18. Available at: https://www.bcg.com/publications/2017/think-biologically-messy-management-for-complex-world

[20] See, e.g. discussion about the importance of leaders understanding systemic interconnections and acting on that basis by Reeves, M. & Varadarajan, R. 2020. When resilience is more important than efficiency. Boston. Consulting Group, January 30. Available at: https://www.bcg.com/publications/2020/resilience-more-important-than-efficiency

[21] See, e.g. Bartunek, J. 1988. The dynamics of personal and organizational reframing. In Quinn, R. E. & Cameron, K. S. (Eds.). Paradox and transformation: Toward a theory of change in organization and management. Cambridge, MA:

Ballinger: 137-162; Paroutis, S., Heracleous, L. & Angwin, D. 2016. Practicing strategy. London: Sage, chapter 2 on Chief Strategy Officers; Tushman, M. L., Smith, W. K. & Binns, A. 2011. The ambidextrous CEO. Harvard Business Review, June, 74-80.

[22] CBInsights, 2017. Apple AM&A timeline: Acquisitions in AR/VR, AI, & computer vision stand out. June 6. Available at: https://www.cbinsights.com/research/apple-acquisitions-ai-ar-vr-healthcare-timeline/

[23] Heracleous, L., 2013, Quantum Strategy at Apple Inc, Organizational Dynamics, 42, 92-99.

[24] Adaptability is associated with higher performance, as the Boston Consulting Group has shown: Reeves, M., Love, C. & Mathur, N. 2012. The most adaptive companies 2012. Winning in an age of turbulence. Boston Consulting Group, August. Available at: https://mkt-bcg-com-public-images.s3.amazonaws.com/public-pdfs/legacy-documents/file112829.pdf

[25] Heracleous, L. 2018. How to make your firm more agile. Core: 51. Prange, C. & Heracleous, L. (Eds.) 2018. Agility.X: How organizations thrive in unpredictable times. Cambridge: Cambridge University Press.

[26] Heracleous, L., Terrier, D. & Gonzalez, S. 2018. The reinvention of NASA. Harvard Business Review, April 23. Available at: https://hbr.org/2018/04/the-reinvention-of-nasa; Heracleous, L., Terrier, D.& Gonzalez, S. 2019. NASA's capability evolution toward commercial space. Space Policy, 50: 1-4.

[27] Peppers, D., 2016, How 3M lost (and found) its innovation mojo. Inc., Source: http://www.inc.com/linkedin/don-peppers/downside-six-sigma-don-peppers.html, accessed on 29 Sept 2016.

[28] Morris, B., 2006, The new rules, Fortune, Source: http://archive.fortune.com/magazines/fortune/fortune_arc hive/2006/07/24/8381625/index.htm, accessed on 29 Sept 2016

[29] Joseph Schlitz Brewing Company, available at: https://en.wikipedia.org/wiki/Joseph_Schlitz_Brewing_Co mpany, accessed on 29 Feb 2016; Cornell, M., 2010, How Milwaukee's famous beer became infamous: The fall of Schlitz, available at: https://beerconnoisseur.com/articles/how-milwaukees-famous-beer-became-infamous, accessed on 29 Feb 2016.

4. Align but embrace paradox

[1] A detailed discussion of the ESCO framework and the research underlying it can be found in: Heracleous, L. & Werres, K. 2016. On the road to disaster: Strategic misalignments and corporate failure. Long Range Planning, 49: 491-506. A brief description can also be found in Paroutis, S., Heracleous, L. & Angwin, D. 2016. Practicing strategy. London: Sage, chapter 1.

[2] Heracleous, L. 2000. When local beat global: The Chinese beer industry, Business Strategy Review. 12(3): 37-45; Heracleous, L., 2013. The Chinese beer industry (A): Demise of foreign competitors. In Singh, K., Pangarkar, N. & Heracleous, L., Business Strategy in Asia, Cengage Learning Asia, 105-112.

[3] Kerr, S. 1995. On the folly of rewarding A while hoping for B. Academy of Management Executive, 9(1):7-14.

[4] See for example Piskorski, M. J. & Spadini, A. L., 2007. Procter & Gamble: Organization 2005 (A). HBS case number 9-707-519; and Piskorski, M. J. & Spadini, A. L. 2007. Procter & Gamble: Organization 2005 (B). HBS Case number 9-707-402.

[5] Mandlowitz, A. & O'Brien, R. 2012. Procter gambled & lost. Ivey Business Review, December 4, available online: https://iveybusinessreview.ca/1085/proctor-gambled-lost/

[6] Miller, D. 1992. The Icarus paradox: How exceptional companies bring about their own downfall. Business Horizons, Jan/Feb, 24-35.

[7] See, e.g., Heracleous, L., Papachroni, A., Andriopoulos, C. & Gotsi, M. 2017. Structural ambidexterity and competency traps: Insights from Xerox PARC. Technological Forecasting and Social Change, 117: 327-338.

[8] Associated Press. 1992. Troubled Wang decides to file for Chapter 11. Technology: The once successful computer firm is $550 million in debt. It failed to keep pace with change. Los Angeles times. Available at: https://www.latimes.com/archives/la-xpm-1992-08-19-fi-5728-story.html

[9] Estrin, J. 2015. Kodak's first digital moment. New York Times, August 12, Available at: http://lens.blogs.nytimes.com/2015/08/12/kodaks-first-digital-moment/?_r=0.

[10] Deutsch, C. H., 2008. Finally, digital products flow from Kodak's labs. New York Times, May 8. Available at: http://www.nytimes.com/2008/05/02/technology/02iht-kodak.1.12519200.html.

[11] Mattioli, D., 2012. Kodak shutters camera business. Wall Street Journal, February 10, Available at: http://www.wsj.com/articles/SB10001424052970203824904577212873966942132

[12] Hardy, Q, 2015. At Kodak, clinging to a future beyond film, 20 March. The New York Times, available at: https://www.nytimes.com/2015/03/22/business/at-kodak-clinging-to-a-future-beyond-film.html

[13] Jinks, B., 2013. Kodak moments just a memory as company exits bankruptcy. Bloomberg, September 3, Available at: http://www.bloomberg.com/news/articles/2013-09-03/kodak-exits-bankruptcy-as-printer-without-photographs.

[14] Knowledge@Wharton. 2002. Lou Gestner's turnaround tales at IBM. December 18. Available at: https://knowledge.wharton.upenn.edu/article/lou-gerstners-turnaround-tales-at-ibm/

[15] Saran, C. 2017. IBM results show shift to AI and cloud business focus. ComputerWeekly.com. Available at: https://www.computerweekly.com/news/450411363/IBM-results-show-shift-to-AI-and-cloud-business-focus

[16] Waldman, D. A. & Bowen, D. E. 2016. Learning to be a paradox-savvy leader. Academy of Management Perspectives, 30: 316-27.

[17] Quote is from Smith, W. K., Lewis, M. W., & Tushman, M. L. 2016. "Both/And" leadership. Harvard Business Review. Available at: https://hbr.org/2016/05/both-and-leadership.

[18] Fredberg, T. 2014. If I say it's complex it bloody well will be: CEO strategies for managing paradox. Journal of Applied Behavioral Science, 50: 171-188.

[19] Favaro, K. 2013. Is strategy fixed or variable? S+B blog, July 18.

[20] Koestler, A. 1967. The three domains of creativity. In Bugental, J. F. T. (Ed.), Challenges of humanistic psychology. NY: McGraw-Hill, pp. 31-40. Quotes is from page 33.

[21] Said Business School and Heidrick & Struggles. 2015. The CEO Report: Embracing the paradoxes of leadership and the power of doubt. Available at:

http://www.heidrick.com/~/media/Publications%20and%20Reports/The-CEO-Report-v2.pdf.

22 For a paradoxical take on Toyota's competitive advantage see Takeuchi, H., Osono, E. & Shimizu, N. 2008. The contradictions that drive Toyota's success. Harvard Business Review, June, 1-8; and Osono, E., Shimizu, N. & Takeuchi, H., 2008, Extreme Toyota: Radical contradictions that drive success at the world's best manufacturer, Wiley.

23 Quote is from Takeuchi, Osono & Shimizu, 2008, p. 2.

24 Adler, P. S., Goldoftas, B. & Levine, D. I. 1999. Flexibility versus efficiency? A case study of model changeovers in the Toyota production system, Organization Science, 10: 43-68.

25 Stewart, T. A. & Raman, A. P. 2007, Lessons from Toyota's long drive, Harvard Business Review, July-August, 74-83.

26 Toyota's Guiding Principles are included in Heracleous, L. & Papachroni, A. 2013. Toyota: Building competitive advantage through uniqueness, in Singh, K., Pangarkar, N. & Heracleous, L., Business Strategy in Asia, Singapore: Cengage Learning, pp. 343-351.

27 Reeves, M. Bergman, R., Gourevitch, A. & Ortiz, M. 2016. Forks in the road: Navigating industry disruption, Boston Consulting Group, www.bcgperspectives.com, p. 8.

28 See Tushman, M. L. and O'Reilly, C. A. 1996. Ambidextrous organizations: Managing evolutionary and revolutionary change. California Management Review, 38 (4): 8–30; and in O'Reilly, C. A. and Tushman, M. L. 2004. The ambidextrous organization. Harvard Business Review, April: 74-83.

5. Alignment and Paradoxes at Singapore Airlines

[1] Ruggiero, N. 2020. Why Singapore Airlines was voted best international airline 25 years in a row. Travel + Leisure, 8 July. Available at: https://www.travelandleisure.com/worlds-best/singapore-airlines-best-international-airline-25-years

[2] Porter, M. E., 1980, Competitive strategy, New York: Free Press.

[3] This chapter draws from Heracleous, L. & Wirtz, J., 2014, Singapore Airlines: Achieving sustainable advantage through mastering paradox, Journal of Applied Behavioral Science, 50: 150-170, from Heracleous, L. & Wirtz, J., 2010, Singapore Airlines' balancing act, Harvard Business Review, July-August, 145-149, and from other related publications over the years.

[4] Heracleous, L. & Wirtz, J., 2009, Strategy and organization at Singapore Airlines: Achieving competitive advantage through dual strategy, Journal of Air Transport Management, 15: 274-279.

[5] Heracleous, L., Wirtz, J. and Johnston, R., 2004, Cost effective service excellence: Lessons from Singapore Airlines, Business Strategy Review, 15 (1): 33-38.

[6] Figures are net profit martins (net profit as a percentage of revenue). Singapore Airlines figures are obtained from its Annual Reports and refer to the Airline performance as opposed to the Group performance. The 2018-19 annual report is available at: https://www.singaporeair.com/saar5/pdf/Investor-Relations/Annual-Report/annualreport1819.pdf. Industry figures are from IATA's periodic releases on the Economic Performance of the Airline Industry. The June 2020 release is available at: https://www.iata.org/en/iata-repository/publications/economic-reports/airline-industry-

economic-performance-june-2020-report/

[7] Based on information from Singapore Airlines' annual report 2017-2018, available at: https://www.singaporeair.com/saar5/pdf/Investor-Relations/Annual-Report/annualreport1718.pdf

[8] Singapore Airlines press release, 29 January 2018, available at: https://www.singaporeair.com/en_UK/bn/media-centre/press-release/article/?q=en_UK/2018/January-March/ne0318-180129

[9] Yu, E. 2018. Singapore Airlines employees urged to innovate, fail without fear. November 9. Available at: https://www.zdnet.com/article/singapore-airlines-employees-urged-to-innovate-fail-without-fear/ Quote is from George Wang, Senior Vice President of IT at Singapore Airlines.

[10] Economist, 2003, Open skies and flights of fancy, 2nd October; IATA, 2020, New study on airline investor returns: Regional divergence impacting overall performance, 7 February, available online: https://www.iata.org/en/iata-repository/publications/economic-reports/new-study-on-airline-investor-returns/

[11] IATA, 2020, Economic performance of the airline industry, 9th June, available at: https://www.iata.org/en/iata-repository/publications/economic-reports/airline-industry-economic-performance-june-2020-report/

[12] Pool, M. S. & Van de Ven, A. H., 1989, Using paradox to build management and organization theories, Academy of Management Review, 14: 562-578.

[13] Rating available online at: https://skytraxratings.com/airlines?stars=5

14 Vincent, C., Boyce, M. S., Strik, J. & Polizzi, D., 2007, Aviation 2010: Achieving efficiency and differentiation in turbulent times, IBM Institute for Business Value.

15 Airline Leader, 2016, CASK analysis allows global airline unit cost benchmarking and strategic mapping, May-June, 62-67.

16 Wirtz, J., Heracleous, L., and Pangarkar, N., 2008, Managing human resources for service excellence and cost effectiveness at Singapore Airlines, Managing Service Quality, 18 (1): 4-19.

17 Singapore Airlines, 2018, Sustainability report 2017-18, available at: https://www.singaporeair.com/saar5/pdf/Investor-Relations/Annual-Report/sustainabilityreport1718.pdf

18 Singapore Airlines Annual Report, 2018-19.

19 Statista, 2020, Average age of the global operating aircraft fleet from 2020 to 2030, by region or country, available at: https://www.statista.com/statistics/751440/aviation-industry-aircraft-fleet-age-by-region/

20 Doganis, R., 2006, The Airline Business, 2nd edition, Abingdon: Routledge.

21 Tuzovic, S., Wirtz, J. & Heracleous, L., 2018, How do innovators stay innovative? A longitudinal case analysis, Journal of Services Marketing, 32(1): 34-45.

22 Heracleous, L., Wirtz, J. and Johnston, B., 2005, Kung Fu service development at Singapore Airlines, Business Strategy Review, Winter: 26-31.

23 Yu, E. 2018. Singapore Airlines employees urged to innovate, fail without fear. November 9. Available at: https://www.zdnet.com/article/singapore-airlines-employees-urged-to-innovate-fail-without-fear/

6. Janus Strategy at Singapore Airlines

[1] Heracleous, L. & Wirtz, J., 2009, Strategy and organization at Singapore Airlines: Achieving competitive advantage through dual strategy, Journal of Air Transport Management, 15: 274-279.

[2] Heracleous, L. & Wirtz, J., 2014, Singapore Airlines: Achieving sustainable advantage through mastering paradox, Journal of Applied Behavioral Science, 50: 150-170.

[3] Heracleous, L., Wirtz, J. and Johnston, R., 2004, Cost effective service excellence: Lessons from Singapore Airlines, Business Strategy Review, 15 (1): 33-38.

[4] Wirtz, J., Heracleous, L., and Pangarkar, N. 2008. Managing human resources for service excellence and cost effectiveness at Singapore Airlines. Managing Service Quality, 18 (1): 4-19.

[5] Rennie, M. W. 1993. Global competitiveness: Born global. McKinsey Quarterly, 4: 45-52.

[6] Singapore Airlines, 1993. Address by Singapore Airlines' Deputy Managing Director (Commercial), Mr Michael Tan, to the Indonesian Business Association of Singapore (IBAS) on 18 March 1993: "Forging a competitive edge – The SIA experience".

[7] Singapore Airlines Sustainability Report 2016-17, available at: https://www.singaporeair.com/saar5/pdf/Investor-Relations/Annual-Report/sustainabilityreport1617.pdf

[8] Tuzovic, S., Wirtz, J. & Heracleous, L., 2018, How do innovators stay innovative? A longitudinal case analysis, Journal of Services Marketing, 32(1): 34-45.

[9] Heracleous, L. & Wirtz, J., 2010, Singapore Airlines' balancing act, Harvard Business Review, July-August, 145-149.

[10] Wirtz, J., Heracleous, L., and Pangarkar, N. 2008. Managing human resources for service excellence and cost effectiveness at Singapore Airlines. Managing Service Quality, 18 (1): 4-19.

[11] For examples of activity maps and associated discussion see, e.g. Porter, M. E. 1996. What is strategy? Harvard Business Review, Nov-Dec: 61-78.

[12] Barney, J. B. 1995. Looking inside for competitive advantage. Academy of Management Executive, 9(4): 49-61; Barney, J. & Hesterly, W. 2010. VRIO Framework. In Strategic management and competitive advantage. NJ: Pearson: 68-86.

[13] Heracleous, L., Wirtz, J. & Pangarkar, N. 2009. Flying high in a competitive industry. Secrets of the world's leading airline. Singapore: McGraw-Hill.

[14] Heracleous, L. & Werres, K. 2016. On the road to disaster: Strategic misalignments and corporate failure. Long Range Planning, 49: 491-506.

[15] Heracleous, L., Wirtz, J. & Pangarkar, N. 2009. Flying high in a competitive industry. Secrets of the world's leading airline. Singapore: McGraw-Hill.

7. Janus Strategy at Apple Inc

[1] This chapter draws from Heracleous, L. 2013. Quantum strategy at Apple Inc. Organization Dynamics, 42: 92-99; and from Heracleous, L. and Papachroni, A. 2012. Strategic leadership and innovation at Apple Inc. Case Center, Reference number 309-038-1; and Heracleous, L. 2012. Strategic leadership and innovation at Apple Inc., Case Center, Case Teaching Note Reference number 309-038-8.

[2] Apple Inc Annual Report 2019, available at: https://s2.q4cdn.com/470004039/files/doc_financials/201

9/ar/_10-K-2019-(As-Filed).pdf

[3] Boston Consulting Group, 2020. The most innovative companies ranking over time, June 22. Available at: https://www.bcg.com/publications/2020/most-innovative-companies/data-overview

[4] Thomke, S. & Feinberg, B. 2012. Design thinking and innovation at Apple. Harvard Business School Case 9-609-066.

[5] CBInsights, 2017. Apple AM&A timeline: Acquisitions in AR/VR, AI, & computer vision stand out. June 6. Available at: https://www.cbinsights.com/research/apple-acquisitions-ai-ar-vr-healthcare-timeline/

[6] Fiegerman, S. 2014. Tim Cook's philosophy at Apple, in his own words. September 17. Available at: https://mashable.com/2014/09/17/tim-cooks-apple

[7] Tim Cook's actions to enhance efficiency at Apple are described in Burrows, P. 2000. Yes, Steve, you fixed it. Congrats! Now what's act two? Business Week, July 31st. Available at: https://www.bloomberg.com/news/articles/2000-07-30/apple

[8] Bloomberg Businessweek. 2006. Steve Jobs' magic kingdom, Feb 6. Available at: https://www.bloomberg.com/news/articles/2006-02-05/steve-jobs-magic-kingdom

[9] Jobs, S. 2010. Interview at D8 Conference. Available at: http://allthingsd.com/20100607/steve-jobs-at-d8-the-full-uncut- interview/ See also Lashinsky, A., 2011, How Apple works: Inside the world's biggest startup, May 9, Fortune. Available at: https://fortune.com/2011/05/09/inside-apple/

[10] Strategy+Business, 2018. What the top innovators get right. October 30. Available at: https://www.strategy-

business.com/feature/What-the-Top-Innovators-Get-Right?gko=e7cf9

[11] Fiegerman, S. 2014. Tim Cook's philosophy at Apple, in his own words. September 17. Available at: https://mashable.com/2014/09/17/tim-cooks-apple

[12] Metrics data from CSI Market as at December 2019. Available at: https://csimarket.com/

[13] Porter, M. E. 2008. The five competitive forces that shape strategy. Harvard Business Review, January: 2-18.

8. Strategic agility at NASA

[1] This chapter draws from Heracleous, L., Terrier, D. & Gonzalez, S. 2018. The reinvention of NASA. Harvard Business Review, April 23. Available at: https://hbr.org/2018/04/the-reinvention-of-nasa and from Heracleous, L., Terrier, D.& Gonzalez, S. 2019. NASA's capability evolution toward commercial space. Space Policy, 50: 1-4.

[2] NASA Budget History, Lunar and Planetary Institute. Available at: https://www.lpi.usra.edu/exploration/multimedia/NASABudgetHistory.pdf

[3] Roberts, T. G. 2020. History of the NASA budget. Aerospace Security, May 20. Available at: https://aerospace.csis.org/data/history-nasa-budget/

[4] Amadeo, K. 2020. NASA budget, current funding, history, and economic impact. The Balance, April 17. Available at: https://www.thebalance.com/nasa-budget-current-funding-and-history-3306321

[5] Space Foundation. 2020. State of space 2020: A summary. Available at:

https://www.spacefoundation.org/2020/02/25/state-of-space-2020-a-summary/

[6] Space Foundation. 2019 Report. Available at: https://www.spacefoundation.org/wp-content/uploads/2020/02/SpaceFoundation_2019_Report.pdf

[7] Morgan Stanley. 2020. Space: Investing in the final frontier. July 24. Available at: https://www.morganstanley.com/ideas/investing-in-space

[8] The Apollo project timeline was from 1961 to 1972; the traditional model continued till the early 1990s when the International Space Station started being built.

[9] NASA. How long would a trip to Mars take? Available at: https://image.gsfc.nasa.gov/poetry/venus/q2811.html

[10] The whole program cost was US$113.7bn (not adjusted for inflation), and the cost of a single flight in 2010 was $775m. For more information see: https://www.nasa.gov/pdf/566250main_SHUTTLE%20ERA%20FACTS_040412.pdf When the shuttle plan was pitched to Congress, the idea was that these would be low cost flights of as low as US$20m each. For more information see: https://www.space.com/12166-space-shuttle-program-cost-promises-209-billion.html Five shuttle systems were built with a projected life of 100 flights each, for a total of 500 flights. They were retired after a total of 135 flights.

[11] NASA. 2020. NASA to provide coverage of astronauts' return from space station on SpaceX commercial crew test flight. Available at: https://www.nasa.gov/press-release/nasa-to-provide-coverage-of-astronauts-return-from-space-station-on-spacex-commercial

[12] Space Foundation. 2019. Space Foundation's The Space Report 2009 reveals industry growth to $257 billion in global space revenues for 2008. Available at:

https://www.spacefoundation.org/2009/03/30/space-foundations-the-space-report-2009-reveals-industry-growth-to-257-billion-in-global-space-revenues-for-2008/

13 NASA. 2019. NASA and Uber test system for future urban air transport. October 3. Available at: https://www.nasa.gov/feature/ames/nasa-and-uber-test-system-for-future-urban-air-transport

14 NASA. 2019. Google and NASA achieve quantum supremacy. October 23. Available at: https://www.nasa.gov/feature/ames/quantum-supremacy/

15 Delbert, C. 2020. Is NASA actually working on a warp drive? Popular Mechanics, May 12. Available at: https://www.popularmechanics.com/science/a32449240/nasa-warp-drive-space-time/; White, H. 2011. Warp field mechanics 101. Paper delivered at the 100 Year Starship Symposium, Orlando, Fl. Available at: https://ntrs.nasa.gov/archive/nasa/casi.ntrs.nasa.gov/20110015936.pdf

16 Wall. M. 2020. "By any means necessary". Vice President Pence urges NASA on moon-Mars goal. Space.com, February 19. Available at: https://www.space.com/vp-pence-pushes-nasa-moon-mars-goal.html

17 Heracleous, L. 2018. How to make your firm more agile. Core: 51. Prange, C. & Heracleous, L. (Eds.) 2018. Agility.X: How organizations thrive in unpredictable times. Cambridge: Cambridge University Press.

9. Agents of Janus: The NASA pirates

1 This chapter draws from Heracleous, L., Wawarta, C., Gonzalez, S. & Paroutis, S., 2019. How a group of NASA renegades transformed mission control. MIT Sloan Management Review, April 5. Available at:

https://sloanreview.mit.edu/article/how-a-group-of-nasa-renegades-transformed-mission-control/

[2] Muratore, J. F., Heindel, T., Murhy, T., Rasmussen, A., & McFarland, R. 1990. Real-time data acquisition at mission control. Communications of the ACM, 33(12): 18-31.

[3] Muratore, J. F., Heindel, T., Murhy, T., Rasmussen, A., & McFarland, R. 1990. Real-time data acquisition at mission control. Communications of the ACM, 33(12): 18-31. Quote from page 21.

[4] Muratore, J. F. 2008. NASA Johnson Space Center Oral History Project, interviewed by R. Wright, 14 May. [online]. Available at https://www.jsc.nasa.gov/history/oral_histories/SSP/MuratoreJF_5-14-08.pdf

[5] Kranz, E. F. 2011. NASA Johnson Space Center Oral History Project, interviewed by Ross-Nazzal, 7 December.

[6] Muratore, J. F., Heindel, T., Murhy, T., Rasmussen, A., & McFarland, R. 1990. Real-time data acquisition at mission control. Communications of the ACM, 33(12): 18-31. Quote from page 21.

[7] Waldrop, M. M. 1989. NASA flight controllers become AI pioneers. Science, 244(4908): 1044-1045.

[8] Heracleous, L., Yniquez, C. & Gonzalez, S. 2019. Ambidexterity as historically embedded process: Evidence from NASA, 1958 to 2016. Journal of Applied Behavioral Science, 55: 161-189.

[9] Muratore, J. F. 1991. Real time data system (RTDS), May 18. Mission Operations Directorate – Reconfiguration Management Division. [online]. Accessed at https://ntrs.nasa.gov/archive/nasa/casi.ntrs.nasa.gov/19920002801.pdf

[10] The photo and patches are materials collected by Dr Christina Wawarta during ethnographic research at the Johnson Space Center.

[11] Space News Roundup, 1994, "Pirates" reap awards, honors. Volume 33, Number 38, 7 October, p. 4.

[12] NASA Procurement in the Earth-Space Economy. 1996. Hearing before the Committee on Science, U.S. House of Representatives, One Hundred Fourth Congress, First Session, November 8, 1995. No. 33. US Government Printing Office, Washington. ISBN 0-16-052423-7. Quote is from pages 163-164.

[13] Pascale, R., Sternin, J., Sternin, M., 2010. The power of positive deviance: How unlikely innovators solve the world's toughest problems. Harvard Business School Press.

[14] Hamel, G. 2000. Waking up IBM: How a gang of unlikely rebels transformed Big Blue. Harvard Business Review, 78(4): 137-144.

[15] Rich. B. R. & Janos, L. 1994. Skunkworks. London: Sphere.

[16] Elliot, J. 2012. Leading Apple with Steve Jobs: Management lessons from a controversial genius. Hoboken, NJ: Wiley.

[17] These are key ideas of adaptive leadership. See, e.g. Heifetz, R. A. & Laurie, D. L. 2001. The work of leadership. Harvard Business Review, December, 37-47; Torres, R., Reeves, M. & Love, C. 2010. Adaptive leadership. Boston Consulting Group, December 13. Available at: https://www.bcg.com/publications/2010/leadership-engagement-culture-adaptive-leadership

10. Playing with Janus: Xerox and PARC

[1] This chapter, particularly the discussion of the reasons for which Xerox failed to commercialize many of PARC's outstanding inventions draws from Heracleous, L., Papachroni, A., Andriopoulos , C. & Mando, G. 2017. Structural ambidexterity and competency traps: Insights from Xerox PARC. Technological Forecasting & Social Change, 11: 327-338.

[2] George, B., McLean, A., 2010. Anne Mulcahy: Leading Xerox through the Perfect Storm. Harvard Business School Publishing, Case Reference no. 9-405-050.

[3] The story of PARC's founding and early days is given by George Pake, the first director of the lab in Pake, G. 1985. Research at Xerox PARC: A founder's assessment. IEEE Spectrum, October: 54-61.

[4] Fong, G. R. 2001. ARPA Does windows: the defense underpinning of the PC revolution. Business and Politics, 3(3): 213-237.

[5] Pake, G. 1985. Research at Xerox PARC: A founder's assessment. IEEE Spectrum, October: 54-61. Quote from page 54.

[6] Hiltzik, M., 2000. Dealers of lightning. Xerox PARC and the dawn of the computer age. NY: HarperCollins. Quote from page 153.

[7] Pake, G. 1985. Research at Xerox PARC: A founder's assessment. IEEE Spectrum, October: 54-61. Quote from page 54. Quote from page 56.

[8] Xerox's process for handling technology spin-offs has been described in Chesbrough, H.W. 2002. Graceful exits and foregone opportunities: Xerox's management of its technology spin-off companies. Business History Review, 76: 803-837.

[9] Chesbrough, H. W. 2003. The governance and performance of Xerox's technology spin-off companies. Research Policy, 32: 403-421.

[10] Chesbrough, H. W. 2003. The governance and performance of Xerox's technology spin-off companies. Research Policy, 32: 403-421.

[11] Chesbrough, H. & Rosenbloom, R. S. 2002. The role of business model in capturing value from innovation: evidence from Xerox Corporation's technology spin-off companies. Industrial and Corporate change, 11: 529-555.

[12] See, e.g. Smith, D. & Alexander, R. 1988. Fumbling the Future: How Xerox invented, then ignored, the first personal computer. NY: William Morrow.

[13] Abell, D. F. 1999. Competing for today while preparing for tomorrow. Sloan Management Review, Spring: 73-81.

[14] Prahalad, C. K. & Bettis, R. A. 1986. The dominant logic: a new linkage between diversity and performance. Strategic Management Journal, 7: 485-501.

[15] Uttal, B., 1981. Xerox Xooms towards the office of the future. Fortune, May 18, pp. 44-52. Available at: https://guidebookgallery.org/articles/Xeroxxoomstowardtheofficeofthefuture.

[16] Chesbrough, H. & Rosenbloom, R. S. 2002. The role of business model in capturing value from innovation: evidence from Xerox Corporation's technology spin-off companies. Industrial and Corporate change, 11: 529-555. Quote is from page 538.

[17] Kearns D. T. & Nadler, D. A. 1992. Prophets in the dark: How Xerox reinvented itself and beat back the Japanese. NY: Harper Business. Quote is from page 88.

[18] Brooks, J. 1969. Business adventures. NY: Weybright and Talley. Quote is from page 17.

[19] Pake, G. 1986. From research to innovation at Xerox: A manager's principles and some examples. In Research on Technological Innovation, Management and Policy, R. Rosenbloom (ed.): 1-32. Greenwich: Cambridge university Press. Quote from page 25.

[20] Uttal, B., 1983. The lab that ran away from Xerox. Fortune, 108(5): 97-100.

[21] Tushman, M. L. & O'Reilly, C. A. 1996, Ambidextrous organizations: Managing evolutionary and revolutionary change, California Management Review, 38 (4): 8–30; O'Reilly, C. A. & Tushman, M. L. 2004, The ambidextrous organization, Harvard Business Review, April: 2-9.

[22] Brown, J. S. & Euchner, J. 2012. The evolution of innovation: An interview with John Seely Brown. Research-Technology Management, Sept-Oct: 18-23. Quote is from page 18.

[23] Gladwell, M. 2011. Creation Myth: Xerox PARC, Apple, and the truth about innovation. The New Yorker. Available at: https://www.newyorker.com/magazine/2011/05/16/creation-myth

[24] Hiltzik, M., 2000. Dealers of lightning. Xerox PARC and the dawn of the computer age. NY: HarperCollins. See pages 263-264.

[25] Smith, D. & Alexander, R. 1988. Fumbling the future. 1st ed. New York: W. Morrow. Quote from page 170.

[26] Hiltzik, M., 2000. Dealers of lightning. Xerox PARC and the dawn of the computer age. NY: HarperCollins. Quote from page 327.

[27] Chesbrough, H.W. 2002. Graceful exits and foregone opportunities: Xerox's management of its technology spin-off

companies. Business History Review, 76: 803-837. Quote from page 818.

[28] Hiltzik, M., 2000. Dealers of lightning. Xerox PARC and the dawn of the computer age. NY: HarperCollins. See page 200.

[29] Uttal, B., 1983. The lab that ran away from Xerox. Fortune, 108(5): 97-100.

[30] Chesbrough, H. & Rosenbloom, R. S. 2002. The role of business model in capturing value from innovation: evidence from Xerox Corporation's technology spin-off companies. Industrial and Corporate change, 11: 529-555. Quote is from page 540.

[31] Hiltzik, M., 2000. Dealers of lightning. Xerox PARC and the dawn of the computer age. NY: HarperCollins. See page 263.

[32] IBM Archives., 1981. The birth of the IBM PC. [online] Available at: https://www.ibm.com/ibm/history/exhibits/pc25/pc25_birth.html

[33] Uttal, B., 1983. The lab that ran away from Xerox. Fortune, 108(5): 97-100.

[34] Hiltzik, M., 2000. Dealers of lightning. Xerox PARC and the dawn of the computer age. NY: HarperCollins. Quote is from page 389.

[35] Uttal, B., 1983. The lab that ran away from Xerox. Fortune, 108(5): 97-100.

[36] Goldberg, A. 2013. Oral history of Adele Goldberg. Available at: https://www.youtube.com/watch?v=IGNiH85PLVg

[37] Economist. 1993. Barefoot into PARC, 328(7819): 68-9. Quote is from page 69.

[38] Brown, J. S. 1997. Changing the game of corporate research: learning to thrive in the fog of uncertainty. In Technological innovation oversights and foresight, March, J., Garud, R. & P. Nayer (Eds.). NY: Cambridge University Press: 95-110. Quote is from page 100.

[39] Smith, D. & Alexander, R. 1988. Fumbling the future. 1st ed. New York: W. Morrow. Quote from page 156.

[40] Hiltzik, M., 2000. Dealers of lightning. Xerox PARC and the dawn of the computer age. NY: HarperCollins. Quote is from page 265.

[41] Chesbrough, H. W. 2003. The governance and performance of Xerox's technology spin-off companies. Research Policy, 32: 403-421.

[42] Hiltzik, M., 2000. Dealers of lightning. Xerox PARC and the dawn of the computer age. NY: HarperCollins. Quote is from page 266.

[43] Brown, J. S. & Duguid, P. 2001. Creativity versus structure: A useful tension. MIT Sloan Management Review. Available here: https://sloanreview.mit.edu/article/creativity-versus-structure-a-useful-tension-2/

[44] Abelson, R., Deutsch, C. H., Markoff, J. & Sorkin, A. R. 2000. The fading copier king: Xerox has failed to capitalize on its own innovations. Fortund, October 19. Available at: https://www.nytimes.com/2000/10/19/business/the-fading-copier-king-xerox-has-failed-to-capitalize-on-its-own-innovations.html

[45] Goldman, J. E., 1985. Innovation in large firms. In Research on technological innovation, management and policy, R. S. Rosenbloom (ed.): 1-10. Greenwich, CT: JAI Press. Quote is from page 4.

11. Three faces of competency traps

[1] Levitt, B. & March, J. G. 1988. Organizational learning. Annual Review of Sociology, 14: 319-40. Quote is from page 322.

[2] Srivastava, M. K. & Gnyawali, D. R. 2011. When do relational resources matter? Leveraging portfolio technological resources for breakthrough innovation. Academy of Management Journal, 54: 797-810.

[3] This discussion, particularly the three elements of competency traps, draws from Heracleous, L., Papachroni, A., Andriopoulos , C. & Mando, G. 2017. Structural ambidexterity and competency traps: Insights from Xerox PARC. Technological Forecasting & Social Change, 11: 327-338.

[4] Prahalad, C. K. & Bettis, R. A. 1986. Dominant logic: A new linkage between diversity and performance. Strategic Management Journal, 7: 485-501. Quote is from page 485.

[5] Teece, D. J. & Pisano, G. 1994. The dynamic capabilities of firms: An introduction. Industrial and Corporate Change, 3: 537-556. Quote is from page 548.

[6] Tripsas, M. & Gavetti, G. 2000. Capabilities, cognition, and inertia: Evidence from digital imaging. Strategic Management Journal, 21: 1147-1161.

[7] Smith, A. N. 2009. What was Polaroid thinking? Yale Insights, available online: https://insights.som.yale.edu/insights/what-was-polaroid-thinking

[8] Smith, W. K. & Tushman, M. L. 2005. Managing strategic contradictions: A top management model for managing innovation streams. Organization Science, 16: 522-536.

[9] Gavetti, G. & Levinthal, D. 2000. Looking forward and looking backward: Cognitive and experiential search.

Administrative Science Quarterly, 45: 113-137; Louis, M. & Sutton, R. 1989. Switching cognitive gears: From habits of mind to active thinking. Human Relations, 44: 55-76.

[10] Brown, J. S. & Euchner, J. 2012. The evolution of innovation: An interview with John Seely Brown. Research-Technology Management, Sept-Oct: 18-23. Quote is from page 19.

[11] Gilbert, C. 2005. Unbundling the structure of inertia: Resource versus routine rigidity. Academy of Management Journal, 48: 741-763.

[12] Bettis, R. A. & Prahalad, C. K. 1995. The dominant logic: Retrospective and extension. Strategic Management Journal, 16: 5-14.

[13] O'Connor, G. C. & DeMartino, R. 2006. Organizing for radical innovation: An exploratory study of the structural aspects of RI management systems in large established firms. Journal of Product Innovation Management, 23: 475-497.

[14] Chesbrough, H. W. 2003. The governance and performance of Xerox's technology spin-off companies. Research Policy, 32: 403-421; Chesbrough, H. 2010. Business model innovation: opportunities and barriers. Long Range Planning, 43: 354-363.

[15] Leonard-Barton, D. 1992. Core capabilities and core rigidities: A paradox in managing new product development. Strategic Management Journal, 13: 111-125.

[16] Brown, J. S. & Euchner, J. 2012. The evolution of innovation: An interview with John Seely Brown. Research-Technology Management, Sept-Oct: 18-23. Quote is from page 20.

[17] Srivastava, M. K. & Gnyawali, D. R. 2011. When do relational resources matter? Leveraging portfolio technological resources for breakthrough innovation.

Academy of Management Journal, 54: 797-810. Quote is from page 800.

[18] Teece, D. J. 2007. Explicating dynamic capabilities: The nature and microfoundations of (sustainable) enterprise performance. Strategic Management Journal, 28: 1319-1350.

[19] Lieberman, M. B. & Montgomery, D. B. 1988. Fist-mover advantages. Strategic Management Journal, 9: 41-58.

12. Seeking Janus

[1] This has been labeled the VRIO framework, for Valuable, Rare, Inimitable, and Organized to exploit. See Barney, J. B. 1995. Looking inside for competitive advantage. Academy of Management Executive, 9(4): 49-61; Barney, J. & Hesterly, W. 2010. VRIO Framework. In Strategic management and competitive advantage. NJ: Pearson: 68-86.

[2] Miller, S. 2006. Former Xerox CEO funded fabled PARC but failed to harvest innovations. Wall Street Journal, December 26. Available at: https://www.wsj.com/articles/SB116683961391258359. Original quote is from Ellis, C. 2006. Joe Wilson and the creation of Xerox. NJ: Wiley.

[3] Rothenberg, A. 1996. The Janusian process of scientific creativity. Creativity Research Journal, 9: 207-231. Rothenberg, A. 2015. Flight from wonder: An investigation of scientific creativity. Oxford: Oxford University Press.

[4] Miller, A. 1981. Integrative thinking as a goal of environmental education. The Journal of Environmental Education, 12(4): 3-8. Quote is from page 4, italics added.

[5] Martin, R. & Austen, H. 1999. The art of integrative thinking. Rotman Management, Fall: 2-5; Martin, R. 2007. The opposable mind: How successful leaders win through

integrative thinking. Boston, MA: Harvard Business School Press.

[6] Rothenberg, A. 1971. The process of Janusian thinking in creativity. Archives of General Psychiatry, 24: 195-205. Quote is from page 204.

[7] Hadamard, J. 1945. The psychology of invention in the mathematical field. NJ, Princeton: Princeton University Press. Quote is from page 23.

[8] Koestler, A. 1967. The three domains of creativity. In Bugental, J. F. T. (Ed.), Challenges of humanistic psychology. NY: McGraw-Hill, pp. 31-40. Quotes is from page 38.

[9] Hadamard, J. 1945. The psychology of invention in the mathematical field. NJ, Princeton: Princeton University Press. Quote is from page 84.

[10] Hadamard, J. 1945. The psychology of invention in the mathematical field. NJ, Princeton: Princeton University Press. Einstein's letter is on pages 142-143.

[11] Einstein, A. 1920. Fundamental ideas and methods of the theory of relativity, presented in their development. Einstein Archives, Institute for Advanced Study, Princeton, New Jersey. Availlable at: https://einsteinpapers.press.princeton.edu/vol7-trans/129

[12] Lavignac, A. 1902. Musical education. New York: D. Appleton and Company. Quote is from page 290.

[13] See, e.g. Spitz, H. H. 1993. The role of the unconscious in thinking and problem solving. Educational Psychology, 13: 229-244.

[14] Sio, U. N. & Ormerod, T. C. 2009. Does incubation enhance problem solving? A meta-analytic review. Psychological Bulletin, 135(1): 94-120.

[15] Janis, I. L. 1972. Victims of groupthink: A psychological study of foreign-policy decisions and fiascoes. Boston: Houghton Mifflin.

[16] Mason, R. O. 1969. A dialectical approach to strategic planning. Management Science, 15: 403-414.

[17] Schwenk, C. R. 1984. Devil's advocacy in managerial decision making. Journal of Management Studies, 21: 153-168.

[18] Heracleous, L. & Jacobs. C. 2011. Crafting strategy: Embodied metaphors in practice. Cambridge: Cambridge University Press.

[19] Priem, R. L., Harrison, D. A. & Muir, N. K. 1995. Structured conflict and consensus outcomes in group decision making. Journal of Management, 21: 691-710.

Printed in Poland
by Amazon Fulfillment
Poland Sp. z o.o., Wrocław

62297475R00153